HOW TO
BUY
10
PROPERTIES
FAST

EDDIE DILLEEN

Bestselling author of *30 Properties Before 30*

HOW TO BUY 10 PROPERTIES FAST

A STEP-BY-STEP GUIDE TO FAST-TRACK YOUR JOURNEY TO FINANCIAL INDEPENDENCE

WILEY

First published in 2024 by John Wiley & Sons Australia, Ltd
Level 4, 600 Bourke St, Melbourne Victoria 3000, Australia

Typeset in Adobe Caslon Pro 11 pt/15

© John Wiley & Sons Australia, Ltd 2024

The moral rights of the author have been asserted

ISBN: 978-1-394-25595-5

A catalogue record for this book is available from the National Library of Australia

Cover design by Wiley
Cover images: © piai/Adobe Stock, LadadikArt/Adobe Stock
Internal house icon image: © SUE/Adobe Stock

Disclaimer

This book is dedicated to my beautiful wife Francesca. You've always had my back from the beginning, encouraging me when I feel weak and enticing me to push further and keep going even when it seems impossible — thank you.

CONTENTS

INTRODUCTION

If you read my first book *30 Properties Before 30*, you will be familiar with my story and my strategy of buying high-yield, metro properties below market value as aggressively as you can to achieve your financial goals. This book is all about the step-by-step practical details you need to know to go and buy your first property, then your second, hopefully your third and, best-case scenario, I hope you continue on and buy at least 10. Property is a great way to get ahead financially, and I hope to help you on that journey.

For those who aren't familiar with my story, here is a bit about who I am and how I got here.

I grew up in unlikely conditions to become a property investor — with my single mum, we lived in commission houses in poor neighbourhoods, and no one in my family owned any property (they still don't). Money was always tight. I'm the youngest of three children; when I was born, my dad was 45 and my mum was 41. There was a lot of financial stress, and my parents were always fighting about money.

When I was eight, my parents split up. My father moved to Adelaide and my mum, sister and I moved to the United States because Mum's sister lived there. We went over with $300 and moved into an ugly two-bedroom unit in the slums of Austin. When I was 12, we returned to Sydney; Mum had a few hundred dollars and no job, house or assets. She arranged with a local church to stay in a church-owned house until she pulled enough money together to rent her own place. As a single mum in her mid-fifties, finding work was tough and she supported us on a modest pension. After a long wait, we were finally approved for a housing commission house in Willmot, a suburb of Mount Druitt. For those unfamiliar with the area, Mount Druitt is a low socioeconomic area an hour's drive west of the Sydney CBD. It has long-carried a reputation for crime, drugs and domestic violence.

I still remember seeing the house for the first time. I wasn't expecting a palace, but this place was truly awful. There was a scrawl of graffiti on the back wall, the carpets were old and worn, there was a distinct smell of mould, and it was in a sorry state of disrepair. The thought of living there filled me with despair. I remember begging Mum not to make us live there, but with private rentals in the area going for more than $250 per week we had no choice—my mum's weekly pension was only $180. At $65 per week, this subsidised place was all we could afford.

Willmot was rough. There were domestic disturbances every other night, with police cars regularly patrolling the streets and helicopters buzzing overhead. When I was 14, four houses near us were fire-bombed within about six months. It was scary. They were commission houses; people would move in and out, or the houses would stand vacant. People in our neighbourhood were very low on the socioeconomic scale—almost everyone was on drugs, and they would go out, get petrol and just burn the places down.

Being constantly short of money caused a lot of stress for my mother, who was trying her best to provide for her family. We relied on government assistance and food stamps just to make sure we could eat. I might have been one of the rebels in school, but if somebody threw 20 cents on the ground, I picked it up.

My upbringing made me more aware of the importance of money than most kids. You need money to survive; you can't buy food without it. I didn't want to end up on the dole and just continue living like everyone around me. So how could I fix the situation?

I started asking questions about money and property at seven. On Sundays we would go to church, and then visit one of Mum's friends in Baulkham Hills, Castle Hill. It's a nice area in the hill district of Sydney. They had a big TV that blew me away. They had nice stuff, in a really nice house, and the drive home from their house to ours left a deep impression on me. I told myself that one day I would own one of those nice houses. Year after year I told myself that when I grew up, I would make enough money so that I wouldn't have to worry about it anymore.

When I was a teenager and started getting more interested in property, I realised that people who create wealth and live in nice areas usually own their property. Either that or they own investment properties — and at the very least they have jobs. No one in our family owned any property. Because my family and close friends never went to university, it wasn't on my radar; I just thought that going to university or college only happened in America.

At 16, my interest in owning property took off. I worked at McDonald's and a 19-year-old colleague happened to mention that he had just bought his first investment property with the help of his dad. I was blown away. How had this guy only three years older than me managed to buy a property when none of my family members, friends — or indeed anyone I knew — had managed to do it? My goal of owning a home suddenly started to look achievable. If he could do it, why couldn't I?

As a start, I made sure I saved as much as I could. I was saving at least $200 to $250 a week out of my part-time wage of $340. It took a lot of discipline, and as much as I wanted to (and nearly did!) buy a nice car like my friends, instead I drove a bomb and by 18 had managed to save enough for a small deposit.

I spent hours trawling real estate listings, and I read and re-read some old property investment books that Mum had picked up for me from the op shop (which I still have to this day). I also got a new job as an office junior at an automotive paint shop. In this role I did the daily banking, calculated the daily earnings, reconciled accounts, and dropped off the daily takings and receipts to the bank. Working with numbers every day was an excellent learning experience and gave me a valuable insight into the financial end of running a business.

I knew that getting finance for an investment property was going to be tough. I used every online mortgage calculator I came across to estimate what I could borrow. I tried 11 different lenders all up, but due to my woefully low salary of $26 000 I was either rejected outright or offered a measly $30 000 home loan. What could I buy with that? I took on a second job as a bartender at the local RSL, working long hours in the evenings and on weekends.

After months of setbacks and rejection, I was driving to the bank to drop off the daily takings for work when I decided it was time to speak to a lender in person. I nervously approached the counter and asked to speak with someone about getting a home loan. The teller raised her eyebrow and gave me a funny look. I looked young, but nonetheless she made an appointment for the following day with a mortgage lender named Kathy.

Kathy was awesome. Together, we went through my income, expenses and overall financial situation and I felt like someone was finally taking me seriously. We spoke about the sorts of properties I had been looking at and my expected price range. Finally, she told me what I had been waiting to hear. If the property I wanted to purchase had a rental income of over $200 per week, my borrowing capacity would be boosted to $140 000. I was ecstatic! I walked out of that meeting with conditional pre-approval.

I returned to looking at real estate listings with vigour, and after a lot of searching for something in my price range, I came across one listed for $145 000. My eyes lit up as I read the description. It had two bedrooms, one bathroom, a balcony and a car-parking space, and it was rented out at $200 per week. It seemed too good to be true! Comparable properties in the same area were selling for over $165 000. There had to be a catch. I arranged to see the property that weekend.

As I drove to it, it became clear why this place was cheap. The road was full of potholes, and the 12-unit block was covered in graffiti. There was rubbish spilling out from the six commercial units on the ground floor. At the door of the unit there was a pile of junk and abandoned furniture, graciously left by the former tenant. The estate agent was a little embarrassed and assured me that the tenant had told him they would remove it, but they'd clearly done a runner. Despite the less-than-ideal first impression, I tried to keep an open mind.

We walked inside and my excitement returned. Inside was not half bad! It was clean and airy, with crisp white walls and older grey carpet that still presented well. The bedrooms both had built-in wardrobes and shared a breezy balcony with views of the lake. The kitchen was an older-style wood grain but perfectly fine, and there was even a second balcony off the dining area. The council rates and strata levies were very reasonable. The area was quiet and rentals were in high demand, and I knew the unit had only been vacant for a couple of days. It was close to schools, shops and the train station. It ticked all the boxes, though I was concerned about the state of the exterior and the seedy feel of the graffiti. But I knew the median price for units in the area was around $185 000, and comparable listings were at or over $165 000, meaning the unit was technically below market value at $145 000. And I could use the state of the exterior as leverage to negotiate the price down further still. I decided to go for it. I negotiated with the estate agent and managed to get the price down from $145 000 to $138 500. Half an hour later, I signed on the dotted line and engaged the same agent to manage the property and begin the search for a new tenant. I took a deep breath to let it sink in.

I had done it.

The proud owner of an investment property at 18 years old

The numbers stacked up for property #1

Here is a breakdown of the finances involved for this property.

10% deposit	$13850
Lenders' mortgage insurance (LMI)	$1200
Conveyancing	$1100
Stamp duty	$3500
Pest and building inspection	$500
Total deposit required by bank	**$20150**

The total mortgage repayments each week were $190, covering both principal and interest. With the unit being rented out at $200 a week – it was basically paying for itself!

That's enough about me — time to dive into the good stuff! How can you become a property investor in the next few months? What are the critical rules you need to follow, and what is bad advice you can ignore? How do you go about buying 10 properties in 1, 3, or 7 years? How do you manage a property portfolio? Let's get started!

CHAPTER 1

My 3 golden rules for kick-ass property investing

Every time I buy a property, I follow my golden formula—my 3 golden rules. Whenever I have deviated from this formula, it's not worked out well financially (I share my mistakes in chapter 10). Sure, you can choose to use other criteria to invest in property, but nothing has come close to working as well for me, or my clients, as following these 3 golden rules:

1. **Buy under market value.** Buy properties for a price that is less than what other comparable properties are selling for (it is possible, keep reading).

2. **Buy properties with a high rental yield.** This means the amount of rent they make will often be on par or hopefully a bit more than your mortgage payments and all other expenses; you want properties with good cashflow.

3. **Buy in metro areas.** I recommend not buying more than 50km as the crow flies from a major city, such as Brisbane, Perth, Adelaide, Melbourne, Sydney, Hobart.

All the other principles of property investing do not matter if you follow these three key rules. In fact, those other principles often get in the way of following the 3 golden rules, leading to subpar investments. I want your money to get you the most it possibly can, not for you to waste time on only buying 'a proper house with at least 500 square metres of land'—those properties have bad yields! Which means you'll be stuck after buying one, with not enough cashflow to buy any more properties. How is that a good idea?

These are the rules I *don't* follow:

- It has to be a house, not a unit or townhouse.

- It can't have any strata fees.

- You have to be able to easily add value to the property.

- It needs development potential.

- It has to have at least 'X' square metres of land.

- You should buy in mining towns (such terrible advice!).

- It has to be walking distance to a train station.

So, let's dive into my 3 golden rules in more detail. Follow these three—always *all* three—and you'll be investing like a pro!

Golden rule 1: Buy below market value

The reasons why some properties sell for over the market value are fairly straightforward. The property might be in a hot location, whether it's a trendy suburb or near desirable places like the CBD or great beaches or top schools. The property might attract owner-occupiers who are less concerned with getting the lowest price and more concerned with finding the right home for them. As investors, buying at the top of the market doesn't make any sense.

Buying a property that's below market value is my first golden rule. It means you literally make money as you buy the place; you can have the bank do a desktop valuation three months later where they value it for tens of thousands more than you paid for it, rather than waiting for who knows how long for the market to improve.

But why would anyone sell a property for less than it's worth? People are often sceptical about this part of my strategy, saying, 'Why would someone sell their property for $300000 when it's worth $350000? Why would someone be willing to do that? It doesn't make sense.' Well, it happens a lot more often than you'd think!

Through building my property portfolio, I have found that there are usually two reasons why a property might be priced under market value: time constraints, and property access issues (because a property is tenanted). I've noticed time and time again that if the sale of a property has a time constraint (the owners need to sell fast) or the property's tenanted (so there's less access), it's harder to do the open homes, so it sells for less.

Time is on your side

As investors, we don't have to worry as much about settlement lengths and how long it takes for a property to sell. But for some sellers, they are under the pump for various reasons. Time constraints is one of the main reasons why some sellers will be willing to sell under market value.

Ideally, sellers would want to have more time available to them so they can make updates to the property that could increase the sale price, and so they can allow enough time to drum up lots of interest so excited parties end up bidding against each other, which drives the price up to market value or beyond.

However, in plenty of instances, sellers need to make an urgent sale because of legal or financial reasons, a death in the family or a divorce. The seller may have secured a job interstate or overseas. They might be facing repossession or some other type of distress. Or they might have bought another property and now they have to sell up in order to finance the next purchase. They may not be able to wait three, six or nine months for a better price because they need the money from the sale now.

Though a rushed sale might not be great news for the seller, it can be a great opportunity for investors to make a smart purchase.

How to find out if the seller is under time pressure

Sometimes you can tell if a seller is looking to sell quickly by reading the information in the property listing. Maybe they have a set date to receive bids by or the auction date is very soon after the listing was placed. Or you can look at the property contract and see that the seller has listed a preference for a 30- or 60-day settlement.

Talking to the real estate agent can reveal a lot as well. If they say something like, 'Oh, look, they're holding out for the best price,' it generally means that the seller is not motivated to sell in a hurry. But if the agent says something along the lines of, 'The seller's actually committed elsewhere' (meaning they've committed to buy another property), or they say something like, 'The seller would prefer that the property's unconditional' (meaning that the seller wants offers that don't have any conditions attached, which tend to lengthen settlement periods), or even, 'They need to sell within the next two months,' these are all cues that the seller is very motivated.

The agent could say those things in 10 different ways, but those are the key phrases that you're looking out for to find out if the seller is in a hurry to offload their property. And typically, time pressure for the seller tends to mean that they will be open to lower offers if it means that they can get that property sold.

Limited access to a property can be a win for investors

I've noticed tenanted properties can always be bought for less because they're harder to sell. People are already living there, and the end of a tenancy contract doesn't always line up with when the owner wants to sell. When there are tenants in a property, it can make it difficult for the seller and real estate agent to have as much access to the property as they might like.

If the seller is in a hurry to sell or wants to update the property to make it more attractive to buyers to hopefully get a higher sale price, it can be really difficult when there are tenants living in the property. And sellers don't always want to wait to refresh the property until tenants leave because it can mean losing months of rent and having to wait longer for the income from the sale.

It also makes it difficult for the real estate agent to access the property whenever they like to do open homes and private inspections. They have to run inspection times by the tenants every single time, and they usually have to give the tenants three days' notice legally before showing someone through.

It's not like selling a vacant property where if you ask a real estate agent to view the place all they have to worry about is their own schedule. They can show it to you right away, any day of the week, after hours, before hours, they've got unlimited access to it, making it really easy to take people through.

The other issue with tenanted dwellings is they normally aren't presented well. The tenant, for example, could have outdated or worn furniture. Or they might have children and the clutter that comes with them. Tenants don't care about the sale price, so they're unlikely to put in extra effort to tidy and clean and make the place feel nice. All of this makes a property much harder to sell.

Access is often linked with the issue of time too. As an example, an investor might need to sell one of their tenanted properties due to a finance issue, even though the tenants might have another six months on their rental contract, meaning the purchaser has to take over as landlord when the sale is made. This usually rules out owner-occupiers from buying the property because they want to buy it to move into immediately, meaning the seller only has investors interested in purchasing the property, which eliminates a lot of potential buyers, plus investors typically don't pay as much for properties.

How to find out if a property is tenanted

I'm always actively buying properties for myself and my clients, and one of the first things I always look for is whether a property is tenanted and, if so, how long for. The quickest way to find this out is to call the real estate agent and ask directly. Photos can also be a big giveaway. If the photos show someone's furniture it can mean the property is occupied by the owner, or if the furniture is old or worn or there's a clear lack of care taken in preparing each room for photos, it often means it's a rental. If there is no furniture, or staged 'perfect' furniture, the property is probably vacant (meaning they probably want to sell as quickly as possible).

Not always, but often, if tenants are living in the property the listing will say that it is tenanted and until when. If that info is not there, the easiest thing to do is call the agent and find out.

PROPERTY STUDY: MOSMAN PARK

In June 2023, I picked up a tenanted property for a client in Mosman Park, only 20 minutes from Perth, for $305000. I had been keeping a close eye on the listing, and when I saw the asking price drop I instantly called the agent to find out more.

It actually had an offer on it for $370000, but the seller couldn't accept it because the offer was from someone who wanted to buy the property and move into it within 30 days—and the property was tenanted on a fixed lease into 2024. As often happens, the people that pay the most for property are the people who fall in love with the property emotionally. They're likely a couple, they might have young kids, and they're shopping for a family home. They tend to want to be able to move in right away, within a month or two. As much as the seller wanted to accept the higher offer, they couldn't because of their tenants. They even tried to get the tenants out early—perhaps they offered them money to help them find another place so they'd move out quickly—but the tenants didn't want to move. So, the seller couldn't accept the offer of $370000, and instead accepted $65000 less. It was a win for my client, who scored that property well below market value, in a metro area with paying tenants already in place.

Golden rule 2: Buy properties with a high rental yield

'Gross' rental yield is a calculation used by investors to assess the annual return an investment makes in relation to its upfront cost. It is calculated by determining the annual rental income, divided by the purchase price, then times 100. So if a property makes $350 per week in rent, you times that by 52 to know the property's annual income ($18200), divided by a purchase price of let's say $250000 (0.0728), times 100 (giving you 7.28 per cent gross rental yield). When you are assessing investment opportunities, do this calculation to find out what the gross rental yield of the property would be. The goal is to buy properties with a 6 to 9+ per cent gross rental yield.

'Net' rental yield is the difference between the rent that you receive from your tenants, minus the costs of your investment property. Those costs include loan repayments, property management fees, maintenance costs, water rates, insurance, council rates and strata fees. (Properties that have common areas with neighbours, like units, townhouses and apartments, have *strata fees* you need to pay, which go towards the upkeep and maintenance of those common areas.) These costs vary so much between properties that it's hard to get a clear picture of how one property compares to another, which is why investors assess opportunities using gross rental yields. My cashflow sheets throughout this book give you an idea of the cashflow pre-tax (before the extra tax benefits of depreciation and claimable expenses).

Buying properties with a high gross rental yield usually means the net rental yield will be cashflow neutral to positive, though sometimes it is slightly negative. This is important because having a healthy cashflow over your property portfolio is critical in allowing you to go out and buy more properties. Too many people want to buy a standalone house no more than 800 metres from a train station as an investment, which often has a gross rental yield of around 2 to 4 per cent, which from a cashflow perspective can cost an investor many thousands of dollars a year. This makes it very hard to buy a second investment property, let alone 10. If you were to instead buy a property for \$250 000 in Perth, and you could rent it out for \$400 a week, the gross rental yield would be 8.32 per cent. The higher the yield, the better the cashflow, which is why it's best to buy properties that give you the highest yield possible. And to do that, you need to be flexible about the types of property you invest in.

What type of property are we talking about?

Different property types attract different rental yields. Typically, when people hear the word 'property', most will think of your traditional family house. A standalone house on a block of land, with four bedrooms, two bathrooms, and a two-car garage. That's the traditional 'property'. But when *I* say the word 'property', I'm thinking a house, a townhouse, a unit, a piece of land, a unit block, a commercial property—it could be a studio. They're all properties to me. Sometimes when I show a new client (who hasn't read my books) a duplex or a townhouse they say, 'But that's not a property, that's a townhouse,' and I have to explain: 'Yes, but it's still a property.' *Property is property.* As long as you follow the 3 golden rules, it's a good investment.

The problem with investing in traditional-style houses is that they usually have the lowest rental yield out of all the different types of properties. The highest yields are usually townhouses, units, commercial properties, and dual-income properties, like duplexes.

At the time of writing, you can pick up a house in Perth for $380000 within 20 to 25 minutes of the city. It's cheap. But the maximum rent you'll get for it is between $400 and $450 a week. That yield is about 6 per cent, which is not bad. It's much better than Sydney and Melbourne, where the average yield is between 2 per cent and 3 per cent. In comparison, if you buy a townhouse or commercial property, the yields can vary from 7 per cent to 9 per cent or even 10 per cent. This is because the standalone house has more land value, and the more land, the more the property is worth. BUT more land doesn't mean you make more from rent—if a townhouse within 20 minutes of Perth rents for about $500 a week but only costs $300000 to buy, it gives a gross rental yield of 8.66 per cent.

Don't standalone houses have better capital growth?

The first property I ever bought was a unit that cost me $138 500. My budget (the preapproval I got) was only $140 000 (when I was 18 and working at an automotive paint shop). On the same day I did an inspection of a house on the same street, about 10 doors down, which was listed for roughly $400 000 to $440 000. It was way out of my budget, but I checked it out anyway because back then I really wanted to buy a house. All the property investing books I'd read told me houses were better.

So, how do the two compare? It's been over a decade since I bought my first property, and today the unit that I bought for $138 000 is worth $450 000; it's *tripled* in value. And that house I looked at but couldn't afford is now worth about $850 000 to $900 000. So, it's doubled in value where my unit tripled in value. I share this to bust the common misconception that houses always have higher capital growth than townhouses, duplexes and units. It's simply not always the case. Of course it is sometimes, but smaller properties do much better than you probably realise.

The reason everyone seems to believe that houses have better capital growth is because the information has been skewed by property experts who've looked at median house prices versus median unit prices. Sure, this analysis often indicates that houses grow more over time, but those stats can be incorrect because they're going off median value prices. Let me explain. When you buy brand new, off-the-plan units, particularly when it's one of many in a large block, you usually overpay dramatically. If there are 100 units in a block and they sell with an average price of $500 000, they're often only really worth about $400 000. And when you overpay at the start, they will sit at that price point for a long time, or drop. It is these types of sales that make it look like units don't appreciate well — they skew the analysis. But if you use the 3 golden rules to buy units, townhouses, or duplexes, they have strong potential for both high yield and capital growth that's as good or better than a house on the same street. Of course, it depends on the location—there are many instances where houses do have better capital growth—but in the past decade I have witnessed, time and time again, property I've bought myself and property my clients have bought appreciating just as well, and at times better, than houses in the same area.

I've even bought townhouses and units that I've seen go up 140 per cent within a three-year period, compared to a house going up 90 per cent in the same three-year period—both in the same suburb (Redbank Plains, Queensland)!

Here's a good example of the difference between a house and a unit in the same suburb bought at almost the same time, where the unit has technically increased at a greater percentage (and yes, it did have strata—I actually bought this unit myself after four clients turned it down!):

- **House** with four bedrooms, two bathrooms, two car spaces on 623 square metres of land. It was sold for $289000 on 12 October 2020, and is now worth $550000—a 90.3 per cent increase.

- **Unit** with two bedrooms, one bathroom, one car space on 187 square metres of land. It was sold for $133500 on 6 May 2020, and is now worth $320000—a 139.7 per cent increase.

Affordability has a big part to play in why the unit had better capital growth: villas, townhouses and units are what people turn to when they get priced out of houses.

The biggest impact on capital growth is *not* the type of property you buy, it's *when* in the property growth cycle you buy it (chapter 2 talks more about property growth cycles).

Different yields for different states

Different states attract different rental yields. If we're talking within metro locations, properties within a 30–40-minute drive radius around a CBD in states such as New South Wales (with Sydney) and Victoria (with Melbourne) have poor yields, the average being 2 or 3 per cent. Brisbane used to have significantly higher rental yields, but they've come down as purchase prices have boomed in the past few years. In Brisbane, the average yield for properties we were buying three years ago was 7 per cent; now, it's around 5 per cent.

As property prices increase and the property market goes through a growth cycle, yields go down because rents haven't gone up as fast as the prices. Often, you can find the best yields in markets that have been underperforming for the past five to 10 years, which at the moment you can see in Perth — the market is recovering and heating up a lot right now. That's where I've been buying lately. It has been a very rough market to buy in over the past 10 years, but these days there are properties in Perth that I'm buying for $251000 that previously sold, in 2013, for $380000 when there was a massive mining boom. And the rents are now double what they were back then.

It's happened in Queensland as well. The last peak in Queensland (prior to the one that we are going through now) was from 2008 to 2010. I was buying properties in 2020 that sold for $290000 to $300000 back in 2009, and I picked them up in 2020 for the same price. Prices didn't move for a decade.

Many people asked why I was buying in Queensland when prices haven't been growing for so long, and I'd explain it's all about recognising patterns. After a very long, flat period, locations go through an increase cycle sooner or later. I talk more about property growth cycles in chapter 2.

What about high rises?

Within a three-kilometre radius of Brisbane, you've got apartment complexes and high-rises, and then you've got houses. The area has an oversupply of unit complexes and high-rises, so yes, they will sit stagnant for some time, and the houses there will appreciate far better. That's why I don't usually buy apartments in massive high-rise blocks. But I have bought a lot of properties in smaller blocks where there's only 10, 12 or 16 properties in a unit block, and I've never bought anything over four storeys high. That's not to say I wouldn't, but it would have to be significantly undervalued for me to buy in a high-rise. I'd have to be picking it up for $300 000 when it's worth $450 000 or more, otherwise it's too unlikely to appreciate well and be a good investment.

Golden rule 3: Buy in metro areas

When I was buying my first properties, people often asked, 'Why don't you buy in regional areas?' When I was looking in New South Wales, people would say, 'Well, why don't you look at Albury? Why don't you look at Wagga Wagga, why don't you look at Tamworth?' These are locations with a five- or six-hour commute to Sydney.

I much prefer buying in only metro areas, though 'metro' can be categorised in different ways. To me, a metro property is anywhere that's 5 to 45 kilometres from a CBD. For example, I bought a block of units in a suburb of Brisbane called Archerfield (I talk more about this purchase in chapter 10). It's only about a 20-minute drive to the city. To me, that's metro. I've bought properties in the Ipswich council region as well, which is about a 35-minute commute to the city centre.

It's important the commute isn't too long because that is more appealing to renters, meaning you can market the rental property to more people, and the property price will increase reliably over time because those areas tend to be more desirable to more people.

I know a lot of people that have bought from other buyers' agents and other investors that were targeting areas like Toowoomba and Gladstone, regional Queensland towns that are very far from the capital city. They were buying properties for $400000 in those regional areas with small populations. It makes no sense to me.

The importance of population size

It makes more sense to buy somewhere metro, like Brisbane or Perth, where the populations are around 2 million, than to buy in regional areas with small populations. These populations are 10 times greater than even some of the larger regional towns, and in metro areas there is more established infrastructure, workplaces, shops, schools and other amenities. Local governments in more populated areas often have more money to invest in infrastructure too. So, if you've got $300000 or $400000 to spend, why not get into the bigger, better-serviced location? Population size is important as a landlord as it gives you a bigger pool of potential tenants.

Metro areas generally have more consistent population growth too, including from immigrants and people who come from overseas who usually start off in the affordable parts of capital cities before they move on to regional areas. These greater metro populations make tenancy more reliable but also mean that properties are in greater demand, meaning that property values increase too.

Why mining towns are a bad idea

In 2010 and 2011, when I was first getting interested in property, many investors were actively buying in mining towns. I did my research, looked online and read all the property investment books I could find: everyone was talking about buying in mining towns. You could buy a property for $400000 and rent it out for $1000 a week for fly-in, fly-out (FIFO) workers, which sounded amazing, but there was no way I could afford a property like that. I had to work within my means and look for properties that were affordable, with a maximum purchase price of $200000—which turned out to be very lucky! When mines started closing down, many of the mining towns closed too, and property values plummeted by around 70 per cent. The rental demand dropped sharply when the FIFO workers left town. Rents dropped and dropped, which caused investors to start selling and led to prices plummeting. Watching this happen taught me a lot about the importance of reliable, consistent rental yields, and how essential it is to look for dependable metro areas when investing in property.

PROPERTY STUDY: DAYTON, WESTERN AUSTRALIA

Purchased: February 2023

Price: $340000

Comparable market price: $370000

Rental income and yield: $500 per week, 7.64 per cent

This is a two-bedroom, two-bathroom house on a small block that I secured for $340000. It has a great rental yield. Dayton is about 20 kilometres from Perth CBD, with decent proximity to shops, schools, train stations and so on.

This property was an off-market sale. I bought over 30 properties through this particular agent, who has a family practice that isn't part of any of the big real

(continued)

---

estate agencies. I've built a lot of good relationships with agents like this. They are their own director, or they have their own property management company and they're selling listings off the rent roll. They might manage 250 properties – and when those owners want to sell, many reach out to their property manager first.

The agent reached out to me about this property, saying the owner had just contacted her wanting to sell. I asked her to send me the address. They originally wanted around $350000, and I could see that most other houses were worth $20000 to $30000 more than that. We landed on $340000, which again was significantly less than it would cost to build today.

This property was a great buy. It's only nine years old so you don't have to worry about renovating bathrooms or kitchens anytime soon. It's a low-maintenance property close to the city, priced below comparable properties on the market, and it ended up renting for $500 a week. That's a 7.64 per cent gross yield, which is very good for a house.

The first client I actually showed this property to decided not to buy it because it only has two bedrooms rather than three. I explained that it's not about how many bedrooms a property has, it's about rental yield and how much equity it's going to make. But they didn't want it, so I showed it to another client who turned it down because the land size was too small, only 200 square metres. I explained it's not about land size, it's for $345000 when comparable properties were selling between $370000 and $380000. 'Buy it, get the equity out and buy another property,' I said, but they didn't want to. The third client rejected it because they deemed it too far from the city. Twenty kilometres is not that far, and you can't get a house any closer with a budget of $350000. The fourth client saw it was a good, low-maintenance house for a great price and enthusiastically bought it.

The lesson is that you should only get attached to details that don't matter financially if you are going to live in the property yourself. If you buy a property as an investment, what matters is what will make you the most money, and how it can help you to buy the next one. That. Is. All.

I remember showing a client a property in Queensland a few years ago that I'd negotiated down to $200 000 — it was a great opportunity. 'Does it have a garden?' he asked. It broke my soul. What does it matter if it has a garden or not? Needless to say he chose not to buy it. It's now worth $450 000 (the client who did buy it is obviously thrilled). Table 1.1 shows how the figures stacked up.

Table 1.1: cashflow for this property

Estimated expenses	Weekly	Monthly	Annually
Estimated council rates	$31.73	$137.50	$1650.00
Estimated strata fees including building insurance	$ -	$ -	$ -
Estimated water rates	$24.62	$106.67	$1280.00
Estimated insurance	$26.92	$116.67	$1400.00
Estimated management fees	$34.62	$150.00	$1800.00
Estimated repayments 6% interest only	$313.46	$1358.33	$16300.00
Estimated landlord insurance	$6.54	$28.33	$340.00
Estimated totals	**$437.89**	**$1897.50**	**$22770.00**
Income comparables			
Estimated lower rent	$450.00	$1950.00	$23400.00
Estimated higher rent	$480.00	$2080.00	$24960.00
Estimated cashflow before tax			
Estimated lower rent	$12.11	$52.50	$630.00
Estimated higher rent	$42.11	$182.50	$2190.00

(continued)

The Dayton property

Summing up

The budget I had for my first property was $140 000, and that first purchase helped me learn these 3 golden rules early on.

While others were encouraging me to buy in regional areas, I chose metro. The area that the unit was in wasn't great, but I didn't let it put me off because it was liveable, priced lower than comparable properties and located in an area with high rental demand. Being able to buy it at a lower-than-market price and then to rent it out easily led to a decent rental yield, and I have carried those principles with me as I've continued to invest.

With my first few purchases, I felt more comfortable buying in places that I knew and had already been to, which isn't always the right thing to do because you can't just want to invest where you know. But at that particular time it was a stepping stone, and it worked out well and taught me a lot. Nowadays I buy in different locations, even if I've never been there myself, because I know how to do thorough due diligence and understand trends and any risks involved.

In the next chapter, I will share some other helpful things you need to know when deciding on which investment properties to buy.

CHAPTER 2

Extra tips to help you crush investment decisions

The 3 golden rules from chapter 1 are the most important things to nail when investing in property. If you get those right, and you hold onto your investment, you will do well.

Now, let's dive into some more tips to help you feel confident about your investment decisions. The 3 golden rules are the dealbreakers, and these tips will help you narrow your search field to get good results fast.

Don't overanalyse the location

Property is one of those topics that everyone thinks they're an expert about just because they live in a house—even if they don't own it! And this usually includes thinking that they're experts on the right locations to invest in, too. But remember: your aunt or best friend or cousin is going off an article they read in the news or a comment on Reddit—they actually have no idea what they're talking about. They mean well, and you can nod along while you listen to their advice—but you're best to ignore it.

All that matters is this: as long as you are buying metro, the location within that area doesn't matter an awful amount.

Many people overanalyse property location too much. It drives me crazy the number of times I've shown properties to clients that hit the 3 golden rules, and they've said, 'I read that you have to buy within 500 metres of a train station, I'll pass on this one.' When I show my clients properties worth buying, I say, 'This property is a 25-minute drive to Perth' or 'This is a 20-minute drive to Brisbane' because being metro is what matters. If they ask, 'Oh, is it close to a hospital?' or 'Is it close to shops?', I remind them that the property is 25 minutes from the city centre so it's going to be close to *everything* (those types of areas are usually close to services and transport). The areas have already been built up—they've been established for a hundred years. It's not like the property is out in the middle of nowhere and they're building a brand-new town from scratch with only one hospital an hour away or only one café.

If you're in a metro area, chances are the property has a train station within a five-minute drive. If you are that close to the city, it doesn't matter which direction you or your tenant go in—whether it's north or south, you're most likely going to be close to a train station, or some other form of transport, as well as close enough to shops, schools and other amenities.

There's a lot of misinformation out there—a lot of experts touting the best spot to buy in. You're better off sticking to the 3 golden rules and ignoring advice like 'You've got to be 500 metres from a train station or 500 metres from a shopping centre,' or whatever else you hear somewhere from someone who may or may not know what they're talking about.

Location matters a lot on a macro level, and it's one of my golden rules: you have to buy metro to have a reliable investment. But on a micro level, it doesn't matter *where* you buy within that 40-minute radius of the CBD (as long as the property also adheres to the other two golden rules).

But don't some suburbs perform better than others?

When I ask people in Sydney, 'Which suburbs do you think have grown the most in the past 30 years?', they will always say, 'I think the North Shore has grown the most, or Bondi or Vaucluse, or one of those other really expensive suburbs.'

In reality, property prices in all states have performed very similarly over the past 30 years (see table 2.1). If you were to compare prices suburb by suburb, you'd find they looked very similar to state-by-state price comparisons.

Table 2.1: median capital city house prices

City	1990	2023	Average growth
Sydney	$194 000	$1 359 936	6.08%
Melbourne	$131 000	$925 374	6.10%
Brisbane	$113 000	$832 247	6.24%
Adelaide	$97 200	$733 501	6.32%
Perth	$101 125	$634 169	5.72%
Hobart	$82 000	$700 629	6.72%
Darwin	$101 500	$585 014	5.45%
Canberra	$120 750	$953 166	6.46%

1990 prices obtained from Australian Bureau of Statistics (ABS); 2023 prices obtained from CoreLogic Australia

When you compare pricey suburbs in Sydney to their prices 30 years ago, and then you compare suburbs like Penrith, Parramatta or Liverpool, which are the more affordable, blue-collar areas, against property prices from 30 years ago, percentage-wise they all show a similar percentage increase. Bondi has gone up on average by 7 per cent a year for the past 30 years. Penrith, which is 45 minutes away in a 'less desirable' area, and Mount Druitt, where I grew up, are growing by between 6.9 per cent and 7.2 per cent a year. The growth these suburbs have experienced has been almost identical for the past 30 years.

When you look at percentages over a short period of time, say one or two years, one suburb might see a 20 per cent jump while another only jumps up 10 per cent. But when you look at the bigger picture over a five-year period, price increases usually equal out in terms of percentage value.

In fact, it tends to be the affordable areas that experience more consistent growth over time.

People get caught up looking at purchase prices as an indicator for growth, rather than thinking in terms of percentages. They might think, 'Wow, this is very expensive, that means its value has grown more,' when actually the area may have always been expensive. Bondi is expensive now, but it was expensive 30 years ago too.

I have bought property in Woodridge in Brisbane, which is one of the places people have said to me, 'Ah, I would never buy there, it's an undesirable location.' Woodridge has gone through gentrification over time. Even 18 months ago people didn't want to buy there, which was funny to me because the houses weren't rundown, they were fine. But it had a bad reputation. Meanwhile, the capital growth there has massively outperformed blue-chip Sydney locations. Woodridge grew 100 per cent between 2020 and 2023, compared to around 20 per cent growth in 'desirable' Sydney locations.

The suburbs that I grew up in, Mount Druitt and Blacktown, in the western suburbs of Sydney, are now very affordable suburbs. They are still expensive because it's still Sydney, but prices in Mount Druitt and Blacktown and other western suburbs of Sydney are outperforming the Northern Beaches in terms of percentage growth (as reported in Sydney's *The Daily Telegraph* in September 2021).

The perfect suburb doesn't exist

It's important to invest with the mindset of the right *property*, rather than the right suburb. There are always going to be suburbs that seem like the hottest place to buy, and you totally can buy in the 'best' location—but what happens if you buy something that is overpriced because of the hype about where it's located? You can buy a property over the market value just as easily as you can buy it under the market value. It happens all the time.

People say *location, location, location* is everything, but it's not. It's nothing without buying at the right price point, which is buying under market value (the first golden rule), and it's nothing without buying a property that has a good rental yield (the second golden rule). If you buy a property in a great location but it's got a terrible yield, it's going to suck money from your pocket every month.

Too often people try and pick suburbs based on potential future developments, like a new hospital being built or a new railway, shopping centre or airport planned nearby. But that's like trying to throw darts blindfolded: you don't actually know if, or when, those talked-about developments will happen. Don't waste your time trying to predict the future—look at what is available now. The 'perfect suburb' is a myth. I've seen people buy property because they got sold on the dream that *this* suburb is really, really good, but they paid too much for the property, and/or the rental yield wasn't there to support it.

I've bought properties in Surfers Paradise, which everyone agrees is a 'great idea!', and then when I've bought properties in Woodridge in Brisbane, the same people say, 'Why would you buy there? It's a rough area.' But they all doubled in value. The Woodridge properties went from $150 000 to $300 000, and the Surfers ones went from $180 000 to $360 000.

The perfect suburb for investing does not exist. You can mix and match what you buy. I'm not saying to only buy in rough areas; I'm saying to stop worrying about nit-picking over suburbs, and look for properties that fit the 3 golden rules. Mix it up, diversify where you buy, and be open to suburbs that others think are a bad idea. Because no matter what—whether if it's a suburb that's closer to the city or further out, and no matter how many bedrooms and bathrooms it has—it's all going to grow in the long term. A good investment property could be in any suburb, as long as it ticks the boxes of the 3 golden rules.

The growth ripple effect

What I've found is that over the long term, in metro areas, when a suburb or area goes through a growth cycle, there's always a growth ripple effect. If you've got 10 suburbs side by side, and one suburb goes up by 50 per cent over a few years, that growth and demand will naturally ripple out to the surrounding suburbs. Regardless of the reasons for growth, it will ripple in terms of percentage growth value. But most people don't see it that way—they get fixated with trying to find out the current 'hotspot'.

To me, focusing on getting into the market by buying good-value properties is a far better strategy. You get equity on the way in (because you are buying under market value), so no matter how the growth goes over the coming years, you're going to instantly (within three to six months) be able to refinance and pull out your equity. That's why buying under market value is so much more important than the suburb that you're buying in.

If I was presented with the opportunity to buy a property at market value in a suburb that everyone believed had amazing potential capital growth (maybe because of future plans for things like hospitals and train stations), or a property in a suburb 10 kilometres away for $50 000 under market value, I would pick the one further away every single time. It's an instant $50 000 made that you can draw out as equity and use to buy another property. Sure, the first one might go up an extra $100 000 over the next three years, but if you've got to wait three years to get that $100 000 of equity, how are you going to buy your next property this year? I'd take the $50 000 immediately.

Where I was buying in 2023

Even though there is no such thing as a perfect suburb, I know people are always interested to know where I've recently been buying. In 2023, I was buying a lot in Perth; about 80 per cent of my more recent purchases were properties in Perth. One of those purchases was in Mosman Park, while others were in Maylands and Baldivis (which is on the south side). I've also bought properties in Tuart Hill, Midland, Scarborough, Rivervale and Armadale.

Some of these are as close as four kilometres to Perth's CBD. For example, I picked up two properties in Maylands, which is about five kilometres to the city centre. It's very close to shops, schools and so on. One was a two-bedroom unit that I paid only $187 000 for in late 2022, and the other I purchased for $252 000.

The difference between Perth and other major Australian cities used to be less significant, but because there's been so much growth in the other cities while Perth remained stagnant, the difference is now much greater. And with inflation and how much it costs to build a property going up significantly over the past year or two, I realised that Perth is a really good place at the moment to buy.

The property I bought for $187 000 in Maylands is so close to the city, and the yield is amazing because rent prices have been rising dramatically. It was rented out for $320 a week at the time that I bought it, but the tenants moved out and I was able to get new tenants in there for $450 a week. It's great value for an investor.

I believe Perth has good opportunities for anyone buying over the next three years or so. I think the Perth market will jump up by 30 to 40 per cent over the next three or four years. But, as long as you keep the three golden rules in mind, there's no right or wrong in terms of where you buy.

Understand property growth cycles

While location (beyond being metro) may not be the be all and end all everyone would have you think it is, it's really handy to understand which areas are booming and which areas are flat. Paying attention to property growth cycles is how you find properties before they boom in value, which also helps achieve higher rental yields.

The property market in all areas, cities and states go through cycles. They don't cycle in sync; one might be booming while another is declining, and another may be rising out of a long slump. Typically, the standard property cycle runs as follows. (I discuss this concept in my first book 30 Properties Before 30 in detail, where I describe how these cycles can be thought of as 'property clocks', as shown in figure 2.1.)

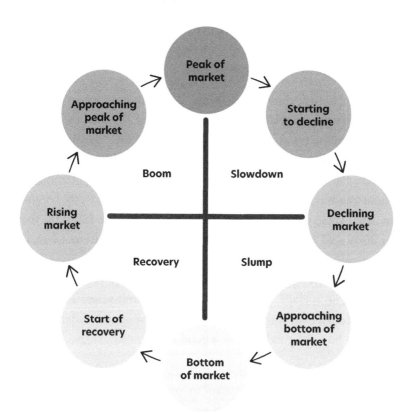

Figure 2.1:   the property growth cycle

I look at almost a hundred properties online every day, and it has taught me a lot about property cycles and the trends to look for. One of the main cycles I've noticed is that in areas where prices have been flat for a long time, a price increase is often on the way. This has been especially true in recent years in places like Perth and Queensland.

For example, a property that I recently looked at in Perth last sold in 2013 for around $400000. Prior to that it sold in 2008 for $200000. So the price doubled between 2008 and 2013, and yet right now you can still buy that property for $400000—the same price it was back in 2013. The price has been stagnant for 10 years, which means that if you snap it up right now I believe it'll probably experience good capital growth soon.

Why do I believe this? Primarily because I pay attention to property prices going back as far as 1990. Over the past 30 years, I've noticed fairly common trends where an area will be flat for seven to 10 years, and then in the following five years the prices double, and then they remain flat again for another seven to 10 years. Paying attention to these trends is how I timed the Queensland market perfectly, because in 2020 there were houses in Queensland going for $300 000 that in 2008 sold for the same price. They were flat for 10 to 12 years. (They went up and down a bit over that time of course, but overall the prices stayed pretty flat.) And in the four years prior to 2008, I saw that, on average, prices doubled in those four years. Trends can vary of course, but this is a useful trend to look at and understand to help you buy in a good place at a good time.

Longer-term trends are important. People often look at what's happened in the past five years to predict what will happen in the next five years, but this time frame doesn't go far enough. If a property's price has been growing well for five years, they think they should buy in the area because they believe prices will continue to rise; conversely, if prices have been flat for the past five years they may decide they don't want to buy there. But that's not helpful. If it's been flat for five or more years, it may be a great place to buy – which is where understanding the longer-term property growth cycle really matters. I always try to buy at the bottom of the market, just like buying things on sale at the shops.

Example: Snapping up bargains in Queensland

When I noticed this trend in Queensland in 2020, I went crazy buying property there. Places that sold for around $300 000 in

2013 were still around $300000 in 2020, but back then you could only rent them out for $250 a week, while in 2020 you could rent them out for $500. This gave them a really good yield of around 7 or 8 per cent. I started snapping up bargains for myself and had clients buy hundreds and hundreds of properties there.

And sure enough, the growth cycle happened; 2021 was just ridiculous. Many places in and around Brisbane jumped in price by 30 to 40 per cent in one year—Queensland just exploded. Now, you have to pay $550000 for a property that sold two and a half years ago for $300000.

PROPERTY STUDY: BICTON, WESTERN AUSTRALIA

Purchased: December 2022

Price: $245000

Comparable market price: $270000 and $280000

Rental income and yield: $450 per week, 9.55 per cent

Bicton is known in Perth as a blue-chip, high-class suburb. It's expensive. Houses in Bicton sell for over a million usually. This place is a small two bedroom, one bathroom, one car-parking space unit. It's one of the first purchases that I bought in WA for myself.

I found the property online, it was being sold by a very small agency. I'd never heard of the agent prior. The ad was super low budget with photos that weren't professional, very basic copy and no photo of the agent. They didn't have much of a website either.

I saw that it had been on the market for two or three months, and it was tenanted with a fixed lease in place. It was on the market for $259000.

(continued)

The flooring is new, the kitchen and bathroom was renovated in the last seven years, and it's in a very low maintenance block. There are only about 24 units in the block, and there's no pool, no gym and no costly elevators, which means the strata costs are very low.

I saw similar properties were selling for $270 000 and $280 000 and I negotiated it down to $245 000. I rented it out for $450 per week, so the gross yield is 9.55 per cent.

The property growth cycle at work

The unit last sold in January 2013 for $320 000. I paid $75 000 less than what they paid for it nearly 10 years ago. That's a clear example of what the Perth market was like a decade ago. Between 2010 to 2014, the market doubled in value, and it's been flat since (until 2023). When I looked at the history of the property I could see the seller had overpaid for it in 2013. (In late 2011 it sold for $257 500, only 14 months later they paid $320 000. They bought it in an overheated market.)

They apparently needed to sell it because they needed the funds to complete another purchase, so they basically just let it go for the bare minimum they could get. Unfortunately for them, they bought it at the top of the cycle and sold it to me at the bottom. Table 2.2 shows the cashflow sheet for this property.

My first WA purchase

Table 2.2: cashflow for this property

Estimated expenses	Weekly	Monthly	Annually
Estimated council rates	$32.50	$140.83	$1690.00
Estimated strata fees, including building insurance	$44.23	$191.67	$2300.00
Estimated water rates	$18.08	$78.33	$940.00
Estimated insurance	$ -	$ -	$ -
Estimated management fees	$30.77	$133.33	$1600.00
Estimated repayments 6.0% interest only	$228.85	$991.67	$11900.00
Estimated landlord Insurance	$6.73	$29.17	$350.00
Estimated totals	**$361.15**	**$1565.00**	**$18780.00**

Income comparables			
Estimated lower rent	$420.00	$1820.00	$21840.00
Estimated higher rent	$460.00	$1993.33	$23920.00

Estimated cashflow before tax			
Estimated lower rent	$58.85	$255.00	$3060.00
Estimated higher rent	$98.85	$428.33	$5140.00

Growth cycles in different states

I have been obsessed with property since I was in my teens, and I have noticed different trends in different states. What I've learned is that at any time some states are growing in value, while others aren't growing or are at a peak.

From 2014 to 2018 Sydney boomed, and over the past three years (I'm writing this in 2023), Queensland has been booming, and so has Adelaide, but Sydney and Melbourne are fluctuating—they haven't moved that much. In Perth, the last boom finished around 2014 to 2015—and it was an overheated market back then. For the past decade Perth has been flat, while other states have been growing. And only now in 2023 are Perth prices starting to take off again. It's not unusual for different states to grow at different times—they have different cycles.

Despite where a suburb or city is in the property growth cycle, you can still look at options based on the 3 golden rules. Looking for properties with a high rental yield (7 to 10 per cent) is a key metric to find places that are in the right part of the cycle. It has to be metro of course; some people get excited when they find regional properties with good yields, but then realise they don't have the population to support a reliable, long-term investment.

There will always be growth opportunities in Australia

Some people get worried that they've missed the boat. They weren't buying in Brisbane or Adelaide in 2020, or in Perth in 2023, so it's over, the opportunity is gone—but this is false. Areas are always somewhere in the growth cycle. If prices seem too high now, don't worry; another area will become a good place to buy soon. I'll always buy in Australia, and I don't believe we will run out of investment opportunities. I simply move my focus around the country.

Tasmania went up massively before Brisbane. Then Brisbane and Adelaide went up, and now it's Perth. But prior to all of that, Sydney and Melbourne went through the biggest growth phase. And it will likely start again, though not necessarily in the same order. There's always opportunity out there. The best time to buy is when you're able to buy. There are always properties to buy, bargains to discover. Every single day there are urgent sales, distressed sellers, a property that needs to be sold—all opportunities waiting for you.

Hypothetically, if there are 200000 properties around Australia for sale right now, maybe 1 per cent of those will be sold for significantly below what they could sell for if the sellers weren't pressed to sell them quickly. You might be able to pick those properties up for 10 to 20 per cent under what they're worth. And that's why there will always be opportunities to invest in property in Australia. (In 2022, there were more than 730000 property sale settlements according to the *PEXA Property Insights Report* for 2022—that's roughly 14000 a week!)

Avoid properties that will most appeal to owner-occupiers

The people that pay the most money for properties are usually the owner-occupiers, people who are buying the property to live in themselves. Owner-occupiers are the ones that get emotionally attached. They envision themselves living there: they fall in love with the tree in the backyard and how the garden feels, or with the amazing location of the property.

But when a property that's for sale is tenanted on a fixed lease for another six months and the seller needs to sell within the next 30 days, it puts off owner-occupiers. They don't want to wait half a year before they can move into it themselves. These are the properties that you should target as an investor because the conditions are best for you to maximise your purchase.

Evaluate under-rented properties

When I started out as an investor I rented out my properties for how much rent they were receiving before I bought it. Real estate agents would say, 'It's rented for $300 at the moment, but you could actually put that up to $350 or $400,' but I couldn't understand why the owners would under-rent their place. I should have listened sooner! It's very common for landlords to not keep the rent to current market standards.

For example, I am currently helping clients buy a bunch of properties in metro Perth for $315 000 each. They are two-bedroom, very modern units in Perth that are worth $360 000 easily. We're buying six in one go (each bought by a different client). The developer is in bit of financial strife because of construction costs and needs cash immediately, which is why we were able to get such a good price. They're all tenanted right now too, so it was harder for him to sell them fast. The average rent they're getting is between $380 and $420 and the tenants haven't had a rental increase in four and a half years. The average person might look at that and think, *They're only renting for $380, which is a 6 per cent yield.* But if you do a rental analysis, which I did, looking at five or 10 other comparable properties currently on the market to rent, you may find they're under-rented—and in this case, all six units could command rents between $500 to $550. My six clients should be able to rent their units out at $500 a week, minimum, once the current lease agreements end. That's a gross yield of 8.25 per cent.

To get this great investment, my clients have to put up with lower rent and a lower yield for a few months, which isn't great, but when you combine that with the great purchase price, and the fact that soon enough they'll be getting much more in rent each week, it's a great deal.

It isn't always possible to buy under-rented properties, nor is it necessary for my strategy to work, but it is something useful to think about when looking for properties. Could it be under-rented? Could it be a better investment than other investors might realise, if they are only looking at the existing rent price?

I bought a property recently that should have been rented for $600 a week and it was only being rented for $300 a week because the owner had bought it 30 years ago and was renting it to their cousin's friend. This tenant was on a six-month lease, so for the first six months I had $300 less coming in every week than I could have. But I knew the tenants were moving out at the end of the lease, so I listed it and rented it out for $600 a week — the price it should have been.

Some investors wouldn't be open to carrying the negative cashflow for six months before the rental yield improves. But I bought the property for around $80000 less than it was worth, and it was such a good deal I had to buy it. Missing out on $300 a week for the first six months cost me $7800 in cashflow, but I made $80000 on the way in — still very worthwhile!

Always do a rental analysis

When you're looking at listings online or are on the phone to real estate agents, don't just go off what the property is currently rented for: always do a rental analysis as part of your research, because it may be under-rented. How much are comparable properties are actually renting for? Search online and filter for the same suburb and same number of bedrooms, bathrooms, car space. Search by newest to oldest listings so you have the most recent ones at the top so you can see the most recent prices. Do your calculations based on a realistic market rental value that tenants would pay right now to rent the property, not what the rent was four years ago.

Even if you're just starting out as an investor, doing a rental analysis this way is surprisingly accurate. Property managers have pretty much done the work for you. They do the due diligence to put those other properties on the market for rent at those particular price points for a reason.

If you want help doing a rental analysis, rental appraisals are absolutely free — they take real estate agent and sellers advocate less than 10 minutes to do. They will generate a basic PDF document and email it to you. You can call up any real estate agent that does property management and ask for a rental appraisal: in essence, you're saying to them, 'I'm thinking about buying this property, here's an opportunity for you to potentially be the property manager, could you give me a rental appraisal of what you believe could be achieved?' And if you think they haven't given you an accurate appraisal, simply call another real estate agent and ask for the same thing. That way, you've got someone who is not invested in the sale (but who may become responsible for managing it) sharing their thoughts on the property's rental potential.

Cut your new tenants a deal

To be clear, conducting a rental appraisal to better understand the rental yield available from your property isn't about getting the maximum you can out of your tenants. The majority of properties I own are rented out for $10 to $30 a week less than I could be charging, because it's good for me to have happy tenants. I don't want them wanting to move out as soon as they can. I want them to enjoy living there, to be happy with the price, and to want to stay there for a long time. Every time you change tenants it costs you money, even if it's only one week of lost rent.

Going back to my six clients in Perth and the units they are buying, I am recommending they put the rent up to around $500 a week, even though they could rightfully charge up to $550. It's always best to be a little generous, particularly if they're a really good tenant. Considering the rent was set at $380 for four years, they should understand; plus, you're still getting $120 more in rental income a week. You're rewarding a good tenant and keeping them in there, they're not having to pay full market price or move out, and the investment is not staying at an under-market, unsustainable price. Everybody wins.

Look hard and look often

I look at properties online everyday. I look for new properties, I monitor the prices of properties that I am interested in, and I look at the listed prices, sale prices and rental prices of properties in areas that I'm interested in. What if I miss a day and don't check in? A great place could pop up that I miss, so I look every day. This research helps to keep me informed so I fully understand the market, as well as helping me find my next property and properties for my clients. You may not want to look as obsessively as I do, which is fine, but if you're new to property investing, I strongly recommend looking every single day for at least three months. Here are three useful ways to get started.

Check out real estate websites

To look for properties, I use all the same real estate websites everyone else does, and I make the best use of the filter functions. I filter for the price point I'm looking at, and I also filter to see new listings through to old listings. Every single day you can jump on real estate websites and filter newest to oldest, and usually, if you're looking at a council region or a pocket of four or five suburbs, new ones will pop up daily. These websites are accessible to everyone, and you can get a good amount of information from them. Google the address of the property and scroll through older links to the property to find out more.

Review RP Data

I also use CoreLogic's RP Data platform. This is usually only used by real estate agents, professional investors, and buyer and seller advocates, because you have to pay to access it. Using RP Data, you can find all the data available on real estate websites, and you can also discover properties that are available off-market. You can also look at the history of properties: how long the campaign has been running, how long it's been on the market or if they've dropped the price at some point.

You don't need RP data to invest well, especially when you're starting out, but it does help you find great bargains. Property buyers like me can help you if you don't feel confident finding a property on your own.

Pick up the phone

Another helpful way to get a lot of information about a property is not just by reading the real estate listing online, it's by picking up the phone. Sometimes you can find out most of what's covered by RP Data by simply calling the listing agent! Find out as much as you can, including:

- Is it tenanted?
- When does the lease run until?
- Is the seller motivated?

- When do they want to sell by?

- How long has it been on the market for?

A phone call could yield a surprising amount of useful information you can then use to evaluate the property more carefully.

PROPERTY STUDY: MOSMAN PARK, WESTERN AUSTRALIA

Purchased: April 2023

Price: $210 000

Comparable market price: $230 000 to $270 000

Why this property was under market price: It had tenants in it and the owner was ready to sell.

Rental income and yield: It was under-rented at $280 a week for the first few months, and then new tenants moved in for $400 a week, giving a yield of 9.9 per cent.

Current valuation: There are units in the same complex for sale now between $270 000 and $280 000.

Because I religiously look online for property listings, use RP Data, jump on the phone to find out more and negotiate property deals every day, I see the trends and I notice if the asking price for a property drops.

As I mentioned in chapter 1, the two main reasons why a property sells for less than the market price is because of time pressures to sell, or if the property is tenanted. And with this one, I noticed it was on the market for offers over $245 000. And then it dropped to $235 000, and then it dropped to 'all offers considered'.

When I first started looking in Perth, I saw that Mosman Park is quite an interesting area. The average median price for Mosman Park is around $1.3 to $1.4 million dollars for a house, which for Perth is expensive, and luxury houses in

(continued)

the neighbouring suburbs go for $5 to $8 million dollars. This unit is located right next to Southern Cottesloe, surrounded by water, you can walk to the beach in five minutes. Mosman Park is probably the equivalent of Bondi or Manly in Sydney; it's desirable.

I realised the gap in prices between units and houses was big, which is a good sign for investors. This property already had a tenant in place who had been in there for a number of years on a fixed lease, and even though other people were interested in buying the unit, they were all owner-occupiers who ultimately didn't buy it because it was tenanted.

I negotiated with the real estate agent.

'Hey, do you have a rough price guide of what they're hoping to sell the property at, or do they have an asking price? It doesn't say online.'

'Look, they want around $230 000 to $250 000,' he said.

'I can see it's been online for a while, are they open to offers even if it's not in that kind of realm?'

'Yes, put your best offer forward and we'll take it to them.'

He shared what I already knew; it had been harder to sell because there was a tenant in there, and they were paying $280 a week at the time—it was being under-rented. I offered $195 000 and they came back with $230 000. 'I've only got $200 000,' I said. 'I can only raise up to $203 000.'

He came back at $215 000, and eventually we met in the middle at $210 000. There were units in that complex that had just sold for $270 000. It was a phenomenal bargain. I showed it to a few clients who weren't interested because it was a one-bedroom unit and they all wanted two bedrooms. So I ended up buying it myself. About three or four months after settlement, the tenant moved out and it's now rented for $400 per week, giving it a gross yield of 9.9 per cent. Table 2.3 shows how the numbers stacked up.

Table 2.3: cashflow for this property

Estimated expenses	Weekly	Monthly	Annually
Estimated council rates	$30.58	$132.50	$1590.00
Estimated strata fees, including building insurance	$62.77	$272.00	$3264.00
Estimated water rates	$16.15	$70.00	$840.00
Estimated insurance	$ -	$ -	$ -
Estimated management fees	$28.85	$125.00	$1500.00
Estimated repayments 6.0% interest only	$190.38	$825.00	$9900.00
Estimated landlord Insurance	$7.02	$30.42	$365.00
Estimated totals	**$335.75**	**$1454.92**	**$17 459.00**
Income comparables			
Estimated lower rent	$370.00	$1603.33	$19 240.00
Estimated higher rent	$400.00	$1733.33	$20 800.00
Estimated cashflow before tax			
Estimated lower rent	$34.25	$148.42	$1781.00
Estimated higher rent	$64.25	$278.42	$3341.00

(continued)

I could also easily bring its value up more by spending $10000 on a new kitchen, as it only has a tiny kitchenette. I could take better photos and sell it for a minimum of $285000, possibly more. Some people might say, 'That's only a $65k difference,' but when you look at the percentage increase when you bought the property for $210000, that's a 30 per cent markup on the value of the property. That's huge! (However, I of course won't do this because buying and holding is a much better strategy.)

The Mosman Park bargain unit

Be prepared to buy sight unseen

Sometimes it isn't possible to physically inspect a property you want to buy, so you need to use other research to help you make a decision. I rarely inspect properties in person; instead, there are three different things you can use to help you know the state that a property is in, which is more than sufficient due diligence.

Rental inspection reports

When I'm interested in a property, the first thing I do is ask to see the property's most recent rental inspection report. This is a report that the most recent property manager would have put together. It's usually a 10–20-page report that shows the current condition of the property. This is especially helpful if you're buying interstate; you want to confirm the condition of the place so you can understand what repairs or maintenance might be required. A routine report will have photos of every single room, and it will have comments about any previous maintenance issues. For example, if the tenant mentioned two weeks ago that there's a link in the cupboard under the sink, this kind of detail will be in the inspection report.

The goal is to read the report to see if the tenants are looking after the property well, and what condition it is in generally.

Video walk-throughs

You can ask the real estate agent or property manager, someone you know who lives in that city and can go to the inspection for you, or your buyers advocate to go through and inspect the property for you if you can't be there yourself. They can even do a video walk-through of the property with you to give you an idea of the condition, which can make you feel like you've walked through it yourself. I don't ask for these when I buy properties myself because I'm not as picky as I used to be, but they can be helpful if it's something you would like to do.

Building and pest inspections

The most important things to review are the building and pest inspections, which are done by professionals who can tell you a lot more about the condition of the property than you can gather from walking through it yourself. Once you have an offer accepted and a contract signed, you will have a certain amount of time to ensure you can get the finance (in Queensland and WA it's 21 days). It is during this time that you can organise to have a pest and building inspection of the property completed.

A qualified pest and building inspector will go to the property, take a bunch of detailed photos, do things like check for moisture, look for previous termite issues, structural issues, cracks in the wall and other things, and then they'll send you through a 30–40-page detailed report. Pest and building inspections pick up more than what anyone without the experience would ever pick up themselves, so they are well worth it even if you can see the property yourself.

Summing up

I have learned a lot of things along the way since I started investing, and there will be some things that you might have to learn the hard way yourself. But, if you stick to the 3 golden rules and understand that property prices tend to have a growth cycle, if you don't get too caught up with the location of the property, and you understand the different things to look for and ask about when you are searching, you will be off to a great start.

In the next chapter, I'm going to tell you about some of the financial things you need to think about when buying property.

CHAPTER 3
The fundamentals of buying property

Before we go much further, it's a good time to run through the fundamental financial elements you need in place before you can buy a property. This might be basic information for some, but if you've never bought a property before then this is important information you need to understand.

Getting finance

Getting finance for any particular property in Australia comes down to two things: borrowing capacity and the deposit you have.

Borrowing capacity

Banks need to be able to assess your ability to make repayments on your loan, so they look at your income and monthly expenses, how big the loan will be, and what expenses there might be when you buy the property. *Borrowing capacity* means how much money the banks will lend you based off your current income, including your job income, business income or rental income. (Borrowing capacity is also sometimes called *serviceability*.)

In Australia, we have different types of employment. There's PAYG (pay as you go) full-time and part-time employment, where you have payslips and benefits like superannuation contributions and different types of leave, such as annual leave and sick leave. When I bought my first 10 properties, I was a PAYG employee.

Banks love this, because to them it's more consistent—if a person has a steady job and they have sick leave and annual leave, they'll have income coming in regardless.

The other way to earn an income is to be self-employed, which can affect your ability to borrow money, particularly if you've only been running the business for six or 12 months. Banks and lenders have different public policies, as well as behind-the-scenes policies, that they factor in when they look at a person's borrowing capacity.

For example, if a person started working for themselves in the past year, even if they are making triple their PAYG salary, the bank is unlikely to take their current earnings into consideration and the person probably won't be able to borrow a cent, because banks view that income as too risky and unreliable. Most require a minimum of two years of tax returns from your self-employment to lend you money. Occasionally you can find a bank that will accept one year of successful self-employment, but generally it is a lot harder to secure a loan if you are recently self-employed.

This is generally the same for contract workers; the lack of ongoing income security lowers a person's borrowing capacity.

When I started investing more, I learned a lot about banks' policies and preferences. My full-time job paid me $50000 a year, hardly an impressive salary, so I couldn't borrow any more. I wanted to continue building my portfolio as quickly as I could, so I got a second job as a bartender, working three to four nights a week on top of my full-time job. I made an extra $700 a week from bartending, which over a year was $36000 more income. Even though my rental incomes covered all the expenses my properties had, I needed the second job for the banks to keep letting me borrow.

This is why my 3 golden rules are so important: you have to have good cashflow from the get-go. It's all about keeping the banks happy so they will allow you to keep buying. If you buy a nice four-bedroom house on 500 square metres of land, you're not going to be able to buy much more because your cashflow will be swallowed up by that negatively geared property.

As a property investor it's important to understand the different banks' policies and work with a good mortgage broker (more on brokers in a moment). When I got that second job, I learned that to get a loan with one bank I was going to need a minimum of 12 months of payslips from my bartending job, and then that bank would lend me $350000. At the same time, a second bank would only lend me $300000, but it only required three months of payslips from the bartending job before issuing a loan. (My bartending job was a casual position, and the first bank's policy at the time was 12 months for casual employment, whereas at the second bank it was three months.) So, I went with the second bank, and bought another property three months and two weeks into my bartending job. Improving your borrowing capacity will help you grow your portfolio much faster.

The deposit

To buy property you need a *deposit*, a lump sum of cash you contribute to the property itself alongside the loan you receive. This needs to be actual savings—either cash in the bank, equity in property or cash combined with any available equity that's sitting in another property.

5 per cent loans

It is possible to buy with as little as a 5 per cent deposit. Many of the main banks right now, as well as many other second and third tier lenders, are allowing investors to provide 5 per cent deposits. So, contrary to what a lot of people believe, you can get started with a really small amount of money.

I started off with a 10 per cent deposit when I was 18 years old, which at the time I though was the lowest I could get away with (I wish I could go back in time and put down a 5 per cent deposit—I could have bought properties more quickly!). And yes, if your deposit is less than 20 per cent you have to pay lenders' mortgage insurance (LMI), but I've always found it better to get into the property market sooner rather than later and to buy properties more quickly.

The sooner you're in, the sooner you will learn and build your experience—and the sooner you will likely enjoy the capital growth that comes with owning the property, rather than waiting to build a 20 per cent deposit. If you try to save for a bigger deposit, you're essentially trying to save faster than the market is growing at that particular time. To me, the market always wins; you should never try to save faster than the market, so use a 5 per cent deposit and get started. Also, some banks will let you add the LMI fee onto the loan, so you don't always have to pay for it upfront.

If you have bought numerous properties quite recently, the banks might want you to do a 10 per cent or 20 per cent deposit for your next property. As your portfolio grows, it gets harder to do small deposits because banks think your financial situation is becoming too risky (most property investors don't follow the 3 golden rules, so by the time they have numerous properties they have terrible cashflow). Because of this, it's really worthwhile using 5 per cent deposits when the banks will let you.

Once you have a 5 per cent deposit saved, you need money for stamp duty fees, LMI, legal fees, and pest and building inspections, plus a small buffer. So even if you do as little as a 5 per cent deposit for the loan, all up you will need to spend roughly 10 per cent of the property's purchase price to buy it (as all the other fees usually add up to 5 per cent themselves). If you do a 10 per cent deposit, you will likely need 15 per cent saved because of the other fees.

How quickly can you get your next loan?

In my experience, if you buy a series of properties in a short amount of time (a couple of months), lenders are likely to still look at the original valuations of the properties (how much you bought them for) rather than do a new desktop valuation (which will always increase a property's value because you bought well under market value if you followed the 3 golden rules). However, you can ask your mortgage broker to do a free desktop valuation as immediately as the day after settlement, and see what it comes back with. If you did a good job of negotiating the purchase price, you may be able to refinance almost immediately.

Desktop valuations are easy for brokers to do for cookie-cutter properties. Brokers have online portals for 10+ different banks, so they simply log in and put the property address into the portal, and it will spit out a valuation. A broker can get 10 new valuations in 30 minutes. I once refinanced a property within the first week of purchasing it, before my first mortgage payment was even due. I bought this property for $640 000, but from my research I believed the property was actually worth around $820 000. To my surprise the desktop valuation came in at $1 million!

Different types of loans

Let's run through the different options you have when getting a loan. In short, you can choose a fixed loan or a variable loan.

A *fixed loan* is when you lock in a set interest rate for a certain period of time, hoping that if interest rates rise over that time, your fixed interest rate amount will be lower, saving you money. This is good if there is market inflation and interest rate hikes, but there's always a catch or a premium to pay if you choose a fixed rate loan. The main problem is that you are locked in with that bank for the duration of the fixed period (which you choose—it could be one year, three years, five years …), meaning you can't refinance without paying a break fee to break that fixed term contract. For my strategy to work well for you, I recommend avoiding fixing your loan when there's a chance you will need to refinance in the next few years.

The other option is a *variable loan*. This means that your mortgage interest rates will go up and down with the market, so if the rates go up, your rate will go up. The same applies if the rates were to go down. If you're trying to buy your first 10 properties as quickly as possible, it's best to go variable first. That way you have the flexibility to refinance with your bank or switch lenders to get the most equity out of your properties that you can.

If you buy with one bank, and then you get a really good valuation from another bank six months later and you want to refinance with that second bank, it's a lot easier to do if your original mortgage is variable. If it is fixed and you want to break the fixed term contract, it will cost you anywhere from $500 to many thousands of dollars, depending on the size of the loan and the difference between the fixed and variable interest rate. Sometimes when you refinance to another bank you will receive a cashback offer from the new bank, which could pay for the break fee.

To sum up, I recommend a variable loan when you first purchase each property, because you may have to change banks when refinancing each property to release equity. However, when you refinance each property to get your equity out, at that point you can fix your loans to secure what will hopefully be a lower interest rate. By this point the property has done its job—you've taken the equity out and you're unlikely to refinance soon, which means that being stuck with one bank for one or three or five years (however long you choose when you fix the loan) is not an issue.

What about offset accounts?

An *offset account* is a regular bank account that you can spend from and contribute to. The amount in that account offsets your loan, meaning you pay interest on a lower total amount, which saves you money and helps you pay off your loan faster.

It's not a bad idea to have offset accounts set up with your loan (they're only available with variable loans), but it doesn't really make a difference unless you have a lot of cash in that account. Offset accounts tend to be more helpful if someone's only buying one property and they have tens to hundreds of thousands of dollars they can hold in the account to offset a lot of their interest. With my strategy, the goal is to buy lots of properties as quickly as you can because you will make way more money buying another three or 10 or more properties priced under market value than you will by offsetting one loan.

Interest only or principal and interest?

Most people who use my property investment strategy are in their twenties, thirties or forties, meaning time is on their side. When that is the case I always recommend interest-only loans to begin with so that your cashflow is better, helping you buy more properties sooner. With interest only, your repayments will be less to begin with. You can't do interest only forever; you have to start paying off the property sooner or later, but you can usually get between one and five years from lenders for an interest-only period. Doing this can ease you gently into being a landlord because you've got better cashflow, which is helpful when you're getting started. By the time you have to move to interest and principal repayments, your rent will have gone up enough to cover the increase in your repayments.

When you do a 5 per cent deposit, some banks — typically the bigger banks — will make you take on principal and interest repayments from the beginning rather than interest-only repayments, which will make your repayments higher. But not all banks will make you do that. And if they do, you always have the option to refinance soon after purchasing the property, at which point you will likely be able to switch to an interest-only loan, so you only have to repay both the principal and interest for a short period of time.

Let's say you buy a property for $300000 with a 5 per cent deposit, and six months later you receive a desktop valuation that values it at $350000 (because you bought it under market value). You can now refinance the property to a 90 per cent loan, which improves your loan to value ratio and means the bank will likely be happy with interest-only repayments.

Loan to value ratio (LVR) is a risk assessment tool used by lenders. It is calculated by dividing the required mortgage amount by the bank's appraised value of the property, expressed as a percentage. The higher your deposit, the lower your loan to value ratio. Generally, you will receive better loan terms if your LVR is below 80 per cent.

To work through the numbers here, your loan amount to begin with is $285000 (95 per cent of $300000). Then, your property is valued at $350000. You refinance with a 90 per cent loan, meaning your mortgage becomes $315000. The remaining amount of $30000 is paid out to you as cash, minus the extra LMI you need to pay.

What if interest rates go up?

This is a concern I hear a lot. Interest rates have risen in recent years, but long before this happened people were coming to me concerned that this investment strategy wouldn't work if interest rates rose. Accounting for changing conditions in the market, like interest rates rising, is built into the strategy. That's why all 3 golden rules are crucial. You need to buy properties with very high yields (around 7, 8 or 9 per cent), so that when interest rates go up you have a buffer to handle it. If your interest rate is at 6 per cent and your yield is 8 per cent, then you have a 2 per cent buffer.

The other key factor is that when interest rates go up, rents go up too, so it's possible that though your interest rate has moved from say 4 to 6 per cent, your rent may have also moved from an 8 per cent yield to a 10 per cent yield. As long as you start with a high yield, you'll always be in front.

What happens if the market collapses?

If the property market truly collapses — say it drops by 15 per cent — as long as you bought under market value, you should be fine. If you bought all of your properties at 15 to 20 per cent under what they were worth, you'll be okay.

This is why the 3 golden rules are so crucial: buy under market value, in metro growth locations, with high yields. It's foolproof.

Your hustle phase: saving for a deposit

Saving for your deposit is about determination and resourcefulness. Do you own things you can sell, like a car? Can you get a second job, or live more frugally? I know it sucks going without, but not buying $6 coffees and drinking instant coffee for the next 12 months will help, even though it isn't fun. I used to eat cans of tuna for most of my meals between the ages of 18 to 20. It was a means to an end. Every dollar counts when you are saving. Now I can thankfully go for lunch and spend money when I like. It's about short-term pain for long-term gain. It's a hustle phase. It won't be forever.

Here are a few ideas for ways you can save your deposit fast.

Do you need that luxury car right now?

I had a client who really wanted to get into investing but only had about $10000 in savings—but he drove a four-year-old Mercedes. He originally got the car with a loan (it cost something like $80000 to buy), and he'd recently finished paying it off. He chose to sell it so he could invest sooner. He got about $40000 for it and bought a cheaper car to get around in for about $10000. It gave him $30000 he could add to his savings, so together with his existing $10000 he was able to get his first property. He bought it under market value, then refinanced the property and used the equity to buy another. He has seven properties now.

Campervan lifestyle

A crafty way that another one of my clients saved for his deposit was by decking out a campervan and living in it so he could rent out his house. He travelled around Australia in his van while working remotely, so he was able to save well with the rent coming in too, and he had a great time. He went on to buy eight properties in roughly two-and-a-half years.

Using a guarantor

Getting a guarantor is the other option for those who are lucky enough to have someone willing to do it for them. I've personally never been able to buy this way because no one in my family owns a property, but many people nowadays start out investing by using a guarantor. This is when someone who own a property (or has substantial equity or capital), usually parents, agrees to cover any debt if the borrower of the loan can't pay their repayments (what's called *defaulting* on their loan). When the loan is set up with the bank, the guarantor is part of the contract—they put their house (or capital) up as collateral against the loan, which takes away any risk for the bank in giving out the loan. Because the risk becomes so low, banks may even agree to loan 100 per cent of the purchase price, meaning you don't even have to save for a deposit.

For example, I have a client who bought their first property with their mum and dad as their guarantors. It was a duplex in Queensland that they bought for $590000. Normally, you would have to put down either a 5, 10 or 20 per cent deposit and cover stamp duty and legal fees too, but they essentially used the equity from their parents' property instead of a deposit. This client didn't have to waste time trying to get a deposit together; they made the purchase and rented the property out for about $750 a week, which covered the loan repayments and other property costs.

If your parents have a property worth a million dollars and their remaining loan is $300000, they have $700000 of equity just sitting there doing nothing. If you want to buy a property for $500000 and your parents are willing at act as your guarantors, a bank will likely require about 20 per cent of the loan amount to be tied to the equity (or capital) that the guarantor has—in this case, your parents will be liable for $100000 of the loan debt if your fail to make your mortgage payments. This means you borrow the full amount of the purchase price, so if you buy a property for $500000, your loan would be around $520000 (if they allow you to borrow the stamp duty amount on top of the loan).

If you have followed golden rule number one and bought under market value, you can then choose to refinance the property when you are ready and you will likely have enough equity to unhook your parents' property from the loan—you will no longer need them as a guarantor from that point. I've seen people unhook their guarantor within 12 months.

Guarantors take on a lot of responsibility and risk, so this isn't an option for everyone. It's a big, serious favour to ask of someone. But if they're willing to do it, it could be a good way to get a head start in investing in property.

Investing with a partner

Another way to fast-track your journey is to combine your savings with someone close to you who you trust, so your deposit amount doubles and you can invest together. It is, however, a more complicated and risky way to invest. I generally think that it's okay to invest with another person, as long as you are careful about how you do it.

When I bought my first property I was in a relationship, but I was 18 so I bought it on my own, and I continued to buy properties on my own when I was young and in and out of relationships. I was cautious. But later on when I was with my now wife, we knew we wanted to get married, and we started investing together.

You might have a girlfriend or boyfriend, brother, sister or cousin who you think would be good to invest with. If you think they are on the same page and want to do it as much as you, and your combined savings give you enough money to get started immediately, it's worth exploring.

Let's run through the pros and cons of buying a property in two names.

Pros

The most obvious pro is that yes, you will be able to get into the market sooner and spend less time saving. If you are both working, banks will take both your incomes into account, which is great because that means you'll have a higher borrowing capacity as well as a larger deposit from your combined savings.

Also, you'll have a teammate to experience it all with. You'll be able to lean on each other and learn from each other. You will be able to split up the admin, and you won't have to make all the decisions or shoulder all the responsibility on your own.

Cons

There are three main downsides to buying an investment property with another person, and they are to do with responsibilities, stamp duty and borrowing capacity:

1. **Responsibilities:** If something happens to your investment partner—if you have a falling out, if they do a runner and disappear overseas, or if they die—as far as the bank is concerned, you're responsible for the full remaining amount of the loan. It will all be on you.

2. **Stamp duty:** If circumstances change and you need to change the entity name on the deed of the property from both of you to just one of you, the government will cheekily slap you with more stamp duty.

    This is something that people often don't think about when they buy an investment property with someone else. Let's say you and your best mate bought a place together 15 years ago, and now they're getting married and want to cash out of the investment, take their equity and get off the title. That sounds great, but when you transfer the title into your name only, you will have to pay stamp duty again and it won't be based on what you bought the property for 10 years ago, you'll be paying stamp duty on what the property is worth now. You might have bought it for $300 000 15 years ago, but if it's worth $1 million now then that's the amount you will pay stamp duty on. (Of course, the other option in this scenario is to sell the property, but this is normally a bad investment decision—buying and holding makes the most financial sense.)

This might not be a reason on its own to avoid investing with another person, but it is worth talking through with a solicitor and drawing up an agreement with your investment partner to factor in costs like this and how they might be covered in the event that one of you wants out of the joint purchase.

3. **Borrowing capacity:** The third downside of investing with another person is that it can affect your future borrowing capacity. Let's say you and your sister buy an investment property for $500 000 together and it has an average yield of $500 a week. A few years go by and you decide you want to buy a house for yourself. The way the bank will assess your borrowing capacity when appraising you for the loan for your new house is that they will only consider half the rent as your income (the other half being your sister's), but they will consider 100 per cent of the debt on the investment property as a financial liability that *you* have. They do this because of the overall responsibility that you hold for the property (as in the first point, where you could end up responsible for the whole debt of the investment property, not just your half). This diminishes your borrowing capacity substantially. A few banks do

have what they call *common debt reducer policies*, where they'll try to even it out a little bit to help you borrow more, but the risk is still there.

Making relationship purchases work

Despite these cons, I think it's okay to invest with a partner—as long as you're careful about it. If you're trying to decide whether to invest on your own or with someone you're in a relationship with, factor in the pros and cons shared above, and also factor in your age and how long you've been together.

If it isn't a clearcut decision to invest together or individually, you do have another way to help get the other person into investing without tying yourselves to a bank loan or property title. You can lend the other person some money for their deposit to help them get going, with a written legal agreement of when and how the money will be repaid.

When my wife and I were together but weren't married or living together yet, but were confident that we were going to be together forever, she wanted to make her first purchase. She knew where she wanted to buy, she had the borrowing capacity and she was buying it on her own, but she was short with the deposit. So I lent her the difference so she could buy sooner, and she bought the property and paid me back later.

In other relationships, a brother and sister for example, if they each have $20000 but one of them is more mentally or emotionally ready to buy, they might decide between them that they won't buy a property together, but that the one who is ready will go ahead and buy the property under their individual name, and the other one will loan them the money for the deposit, to be paid back in the way that they have both agreed to (usually with some interest so it's a fair arrangement).

This way, the person that is ready to buy will be picking the property out on their own and will get to make the decisions on their own. There's no two people pulling each other in opposite directions about when and what to buy. And the other person can make a touch more interest than their money would accrue just sitting in the bank.

It's important to have the loan and repayment details put into a written agreement. You never know what is going to happen down the track, and you will both be covered if you have the agreement in writing. Make sure to be clear about how much the repayments will be and how often they will be paid.

This option to loan or be loaned money from someone you know to get your deposit together is essentially a route to get you into the market sooner so you're not waiting around and missing out, trying to race against the market while you save up.

Use lenders' mortgage insurance to get into the market sooner

Lenders' mortgage insurance (LMI) is an insurance premium (an extra cost) that you pay your lender to protect them in case you are unable to make repayments on your loan. The amount of LMI that you pay is based on the size of your deposit and your loan. Banks typically want you to have a 20 per cent deposit to get a mortgage, and if you're not able to come up with the full 20 per cent deposit amount, they take a bit of extra cash from you (the LMI) as a risk insurance.

Some people think it's a bad idea to do a smaller deposit and pay LMI because it comes at an extra cost, but I believe it's totally worth it because it allows you to buy property sooner. There is a common misconception that LMI costs $20000 to $50000, but LMI can be much less than that. It's calculated based on your purchase price and loan amount (and therefore your LVR), and if you're buying a property for $280 000 with a 10 per cent deposit, it's likely you'll only be charged around $4000 in LMI, or even less. (There are LMI calculators online you can use to work out how much LMI you'd have to pay for a property you're considering buying. Put in the property cost and how much you're hoping to borrow and it will spit out exactly how much LMI you can expect to pay.)

In my early investing days, I used LMI a lot. Nowadays I can't; lenders stop allowing you to take out LMI as the number of properties you own increases. The bigger a portfolio becomes, the more they view you as a risk. So, make the most of it while they let you use it! Some of the larger banks can approve their own LMI, but smaller banks tend to outsource it. It's worth checking across different lenders.

Is it a good idea to buy in a trust?

If you set up a trust to purchase property, those properties will belong to the trust rather than you personally. Sometimes people choose to do this so that passing the property on to their children is easier, or for asset protection. When clients ask me about this option, I usually recommend they speak with their accountant about it, because it depends on the client's circumstances (for example, how much equity they have, what job they do, their motivations for buying a trust). At certain times it's good to buy in a trust or a company name rather than your personal name. However, when you are starting out, particularly when buying your first seven to 15 properties, I personally recommend keeping things simple and buying in your own name. (Or buy in a SMSF, as I discuss in chapter 7.) A savvy property accountant will be able to give you the best advice on whether buying in a trust (or SMSF) is a good option for you.

FYI

Summing up

Getting finance might sound complicated, but it's actually straightforward. You need a deposit (cash), and you need income to have a good borrowing capacity. You can either save, or join your savings, or sell things you own, or use your parents as a guarantor to get the cash. You need a wage to have borrowing capacity. With a deposit and borrowing capacity, banks will give you a loan. You've got this!

In chapter 4, I'm going to share some of my experiences and tips about how to negotiate your purchase and deal with real estate agents, banks and brokers.

CHAPTER 4

Negotiating a purchase

Once you've figured out your budget, decided what you want to buy, sorted out your financing and hunted down a great investment property, it's time to deal with real estate agents, banks and brokers. I've discovered a lot about what you need to think about in these negotiations during my investment property journey, so I have plenty of tips for you.

Working with real estate agents

In my experience, there are generally two types of real estate agents when it comes to buying a property: the ones holding out for the best price possible, and the ones that are keen to sell fast and move on to the next sale. Of course, it depends on how motivated the seller is too, but sellers tend to choose agents that are on the same page.

The first type of real estate agent are the ones that want their stats to show that they're selling properties at the very highest price, even if it takes three months to sell a property for $30 000 more than they could have agreed in the first week. This type of agent really pushes until they get the dollar amount they're after. They might sell a lot less properties overall, but their whole focus is to get the highest possible price for themselves and for the seller. There are some agents who will literally tell a seller, 'Let's keep waiting for six or seven months to get the best price.'

The second type of real estate agent's ethos is, *Let's just get this thing sold*. They like selling fast, they sell lots of properties every year, they're all about making it happen quickly for as good a price as they can get in the first month or so. These are the agents you are more likely to snap up properties from for under-market bargain prices.

The first type of agent will often reject low offers, not even showing the seller if they deem it too low, whereas the second type of agent will tell the vendor, 'Let's get a deal done quickly. Why wait two, three, six months when we can sell the property now?' They list and adjust property prices accordingly.

Tips on dealing with agents

It's helpful to know which type of agent you're dealing with, so here are some tips to help you figure it out.

First things first, get straight to the point. Don't mess around. A real estate agent might have 50 to 100 calls a day. Don't waste time with small talk, just get straight to the point and tell them what you want.

When I call an agent, I simply start with, 'Hi, I'm calling about this property and want to know if it's still available?' If the property has been sold, I might ask, 'Do you have any other properties coming up that you think I might be interested in? Anything that hasn't gone online yet?'

If the property I'm interested in *is* still available, I ask for information that is missing from the listing, such as whether the property is tenanted, and whether the seller is motivated to sell.

If it is tenanted, ask the agent:

- How much is it currently renting for?

- Are the tenants planning to stay long term?

- Do you have a copy of the most current routine inspection? (See the next section for more on this.)

- Can you send me the last routine inspection report?

Other questions to ask include:

- What are the current outgoing council rates, and water rates?

- Could you share the disclosure statement with me (which has the body corporate information)?

- How contactable is the seller? (This is important for negotiating the sale price.)

- Are you able to email me through any extra info you have about the property?

You can also suss out things like how long they think the property will be on the market for, if there are any other similar properties you might want to look at, and if they've already had offers. What they say over the phone is useful information, but don't take it as gospel—the things they say over the phone or in person can change. If you're still interested in the property when you have this extra information, ask for certain things (such as a routine inspection report or a lease agreement) in writing, and take notes when you are talking in case there are things that you won't be able to get in writing but you want to keep in mind.

If you get to the stage where you are ready to make an offer, you will want to ask the real estate agent things like: 'If I were to give you an offer today, and email you all the terms and conditions, and so on, when would you be able to speak to the seller about it? When might you get back to me with their response?'

Some real estate agents are deal makers—they mess around for a week or two trying to catch up with the seller to present your offer. They may say things like, 'I might be able to catch up with the seller on the weekend and discuss it.' Other agents move fast so are much better to deal with. They might say, 'I can call the seller today if you email me through an offer right now.' Then I call them up at the end of the day or the next morning to find out if the offer got across the line or what the seller's counter-offer was.

When I want to make an offer, I always first ask how easy the seller is to get hold of, because some sellers are interstate, don't live in the country or are on holiday. Sometimes you get really excited about a property and then the agent says, 'Oh, they'll come back within a couple of weeks.' When that happens, I lose interest. In the time that I'm waiting for them to come back to me, I could be missing out on seven other properties I might have bought instead.

The main thing is to be confident, calm and direct. Don't be afraid to ask the questions you need answered. Buying property isn't about being polite and not asking too many questions—normal social conversational rules don't apply. You don't want to miss out on a good investment because you were too considerate over the phone. Remember: the agent's job is to sell the place and you want to buy it, so they'll like it if you're direct and to the point. When you ask lots of questions, they know you mean business.

Ask for routine inspection reports for tenanted properties

When buying a tenanted property, I always ask real estate agents to email me the most recent routine inspection report for the property, especially if I'm buying interstate, to give me an idea of the condition the property is in.

Half the time the real estate office managing the rental is handling the sale too, so it's easy for the agent to get their colleague to email the most recent routine inspection report across. Sometimes it's difficult to get the report when the selling agent is at a different office to the rental agent. If the rental property manager knows it's for sale (which means they might lose the management of the property once it's sold), they might be annoyed about that so may do whatever they can to delay the sale. (This isn't allowed of course, but I have seen it happen.)

Agents motivated *not* to sell to you

If the agent selling the property is also the person managing the property, they may ask you who you're going to use to manage the property once you buy it. If you make the mistake of saying, 'I've got my own property manager lined up,' effectively telling them that if they sell the property to you they will lose it as a management property, they might be less likely to sell the property to you. It's always best to say something along the lines of, 'I haven't decided yet, but if you could email me some more information about how you could help with it that would be great.' That way, they know they have a chance of keeping the property management role once the property is sold.

It is highly unethical, but I have had agents straight up refuse to take my offers to the sellers because of this. It's happened hundreds of times over the years, especially in Queensland for some reason. When I call up and introduce myself as the buyer's agent, I've had people respond, 'Oh you're a buyer's agent, you'll take the management on, I'm not going to accept any offers from you.'

Understanding the property management business

If a property is rented for $500 a week, and the management fee is about 7 per cent (which is common), that's an income of $2500 a year for the property management company. This isn't much on its own, but in the property management business $2500 a year can actually be worth three times that in business equity. When a company loses the management of a property, it's basically their business losing $7500 worth of value—and their books won't look as good.

Imagine a property manager has 100 clients, and their collection of clients is worth around $750 000. If they lose one property they're managing, it's not just the $7500 they're losing—it's also how their overall books look to the bank. Because a property management company can use the business to get a loan, it can use the business as equity to do things like buy more property management businesses, or buy a block of units or other real estate. When a property management company loses this business equity, it has fewer opportunities to grow the business or make investments of its own.

Putting in an offer

This is the exciting part: time to put in an offer on that property you've taken the time to research and decide on! But how?

I tend to put all my offers in writing by email, so I make sure to get the real estate agent's direct email address. Once I'm ready to go, I send them my offer—which includes the price, the terms and conditions, the initial deposit, and any finance and pest and building inspection clauses. You can sometimes do it over the phone prior, but always email your offer through as well so you've both got it in writing.

Once you know a seller is motivated to sell, you have a higher chance of negotiating the purchase price down. I often start my offer anywhere from 5 to 20 per cent below the asking price, depending on whether it is already good value at the asking price based on comparable sales and on market-comparable properties. (Overall, I aim to buy properties 5 to 20 per cent below market value, as a rough guide.) If they want $320 000, I may offer $285 000 to begin with. They might counter with $305 000, at which I say $290 000. They might say $300 000, to which I say $292 000. Often I'll be able to get them to agree to a price around $295 000 in this scenario, but if comparable properties are selling for $340 000 I may agree on a price of $300 000.

Sometimes you will deal with agents who don't know how to negotiate effectively. You put in an offer, they chat to the seller, and then come back to you saying, 'They've rejected your offer,' with no counter-offer in response. When this happens, rather than accepting the flat-out rejection, ask: 'Do they have a counter-offer? What price point would they consider selling for today?' Keep the negotiation moving. You would think all agents know how to get a deal done, but it's crazy the number of times I've dealt with agents like this!

I cover more details on the exciting and nerve-racking process of negotiating a purchase price in chapter 5.

Dealing with banks and mortgage brokers

Dealing with banks when you're looking to buy a property can be a bit like diving into a rabbit hole. There are lots of options and it gets complicated. Thankfully, I haven't had to do it in a while as I now have a mortgage broker that does the bank-wrangling for me, but when I first started out, I had to start from scratch and learn all about the specifics of how to deal with banks and mortgage brokers. There's a lot to get your head around, so let's dive in.

Types of banks and lenders

Everyone knows about the big banks, known as first-tier banks, like ANZ, Commonwealth Bank, NAB and Westpac, and most people have heard of the mid-size or second-tier lenders, like ING and BOQ, but not as many people know about the other, smaller, third-tier lenders.

The big banks are generally more cautious with their lending and have lower interest rates, while the mid-size lenders tend to have higher interest rates than the big banks but can be a bit more flexible with their lending policies. Then there are the third-tier lenders, such as Pepper Money, La Trobe Financial, Liberty, Granite Financial Services and Firstmac. They're basically small banks; they don't have as many staff, as much history or as many clients as the big banks, and often they may not have a physical storefront.

As a general rule, if you can start out with a first-tier bank, I recommend doing that. They will give you a better interest rate, for starters—nowadays, some will provide a loan with as little as a 5 per cent deposit—and they can easily do desktop valuations of your property (which is important when you're refinancing in six-, 12- or 24-months' time). Inevitably in your investment journey, you will need to consider using a second- or third-tier bank, so let's talk a little more about them because people are often hesitant to use them.

The pros and cons of smaller lenders

Even though each small lender will have its own varying criteria and policies, as a general rule they have more flexible lending policies in terms of how much they'll lend, the deposit size required and to whom they'll lend. If someone has a bad credit rating, the big banks won't touch them, whereas a lender like Pepper Money might allow them to buy a property because they have different financial products and options (and they often charge higher interest in such cases, perhaps an extra 0.5 or 1 per cent more than the big banks offer to offset the greater risk they're taking on).

Smaller lenders might be different to the big banks, but they're still legit. It's not as if you're taking money from a loan shark or a random person with a bagful of cash; they are legitimate lenders. They're all accredited and qualified, they just operate on a different scale and provide different lending options. Some of them can even offer really good interest rates if you put down a big deposit, which reduces your LVR (loan to value ratio). However, the flexibility offered by smaller lenders usually does come with higher interest rates.

The other downside is with property valuations. Sometimes third-tier banks won't do a desktop valuation of a property for you; instead, they may only provide the option of a full valuation, which in most cases costs you money and is usually more conservative. Sometimes they only have online banking, with no physical storefront you can visit, while their online banking systems may be old-school and not as tech savvy. But there might be times where a smaller, more flexible lender is the best fit for you, so it's worth considering them if it means you'll be able to invest sooner.

You can directly contact smaller lenders yourself to find out what mortgage options they have, just like you can contact second- and first-tier banks and do the research yourself. However, I normally recommend using a mortgage broker; they are professionals who have already done the research and can tell you the best options for your situation.

What is a mortgage broker?

A *mortgage broker* is a go-between person who liaises between banks and borrowers. They help people who need a mortgage to navigate the different options available. There are so many banks and lenders these days that it can be complicated to work out the best option for your situation. A broker can help with the whole process, and they should look for and negotiate the best loan and interest rate for you.

Brokers get paid by the bank that you end up with, so it's a free service to you. They get paid a percentage of the total loan amount—on average, it's about 0.6 per cent. So, if the loan is a million dollars, a broker will get paid around $6000 by the bank (plus a small monthly commission paid out for the life of the loan).

I recommend working with the right broker. Not all brokers are good (just like in any industry, there are bad apples), and not all brokers will support your aggressive investing approach. Having a great broker will save you a lot of time and headaches when agreeing the loan, plus help you save a lot of money thanks to the better interest rate they can negotiate for you. But it does depend on your particular situation. If you're overwhelmed by the lending options out there, you don't know where to start or you don't have the time or desire to do all the negotiating yourself, brokers can be really helpful. But there are times when it can be more helpful to approach a bank directly yourself, as you'll see in some of the following examples.

Brokers don't necessarily have the same goals as investors

It's helpful to understand how brokers get paid to understand why they might want to work with you — or not. Because they get paid a percentage of the loan amount, some brokers aren't interested in people who are taking out smaller loans because they have to do a similar amount of work for less money. They are also less likely to want to work with people who have aggressive investment plans because they run the risk of losing their commission if investors regularly refinance.

Mortgage brokers will often discourage people from refinancing in the first 12 to 24 months of a loan because of two main reasons:

- They will lose their commission if the loan moves to a different bank within that first year or two.

- They will lose their ongoing monthly commission (which they get for the life of your loan).

Say you buy a property using a broker for, hypothetically, a million dollars. The broker gets paid 0.6 per cent of the loan value by the bank, so about $6000. But under the terms and conditions, to protect the bank, there is a clawback clause in the agreement with the mortgage broker. If you switch banks within one or two years (whatever that bank's policy is), meaning the bank loses your loan from their books, the $6000 that the broker earned will be taken back by the bank. If you use the same broker when refinancing the loan with a new bank, then yes, the broker will get paid that $6000 again, and they'll also get the ongoing monthly trail commissions from the new bank (which is paid out for the life of the loan), but they've just done twice the amount of work for the same amount of money. If, when you refinance within the first year or two, your broker happens to be on holiday so you can't get hold of them, leading you to refinance with a different broker, then your first broker will have worked for the first loan entirely for free.

A broker's ongoing monthly trail commission (that the bank pays them on top of the upfront commission) can add up to as much as $2000 a year, so if you are likely to refinance, especially if there is a chance that you will use another broker, you may find that brokers won't want to work with you to begin with. Brokers want to help people get loans who *don't* want to refinance or move banks. They want reliable trail income across their loan books. The more loans they have, the more ongoing trail income they have trickling in. Many brokers sift out the time-wasters, like in any business, so brokers may turn you down because of your desire to buy lots of properties quickly using refinancing.

As a result, finding a broker who will help you refinance can be tricky, particularly if your loan amount is small. I've lost count of the number of times I've gone to a broker who said something like, 'Oh, you can't get equity out of this because the valuations are not going to work,' and then, when I went directly into the branch of a bank, the person at the branch, who was getting paid by the hour, said the opposite: 'We can do that right now.' One time, I refinanced three properties in 48 hours after wasting six months trying to get a broker to do the same thing for me. It simply wasn't worth it for them.

If you're really keen to work with a broker for a smaller loan, sell them on your investment strategy. Explain that you're planning to bring in 10 mortgages in the next three years, and that you'd like to find one broker to handle all the loans for you. Explain you'll need them to do the work of refinancing, but that in the end they'll have 10 loans with you, and who knows—maybe even more. Explaining this might mean they're happy to do the work. Even better, look for a mortgage broker who owns five or 10 properties themselves, as they're far more likely to be on the same page as you and support your investment goals.

So, bank or broker?

Usually the answer is both, at different times. If your broker tells you that they can't get you a small loan or can't refinance to get your equity out, have a free conversation with the bank directly. Call up the branch and organise a time to go and see one of the bank or finance managers (you can also have a phone appointment with them if they don't have branches or you live in a different state). See what they can do for you and what your options are.

Alternatively, if you have gone directly to the bank for a loan and they reject your application, don't just take it as a no — try a broker. Or try a different bank or smaller lender.

Where are the good brokers?

If you're ready to dive right into your property journey and want a broker who understands this investment strategy, go to www .dilleenproperty.com.au and make an enquiry. Our team will put you in touch with the mortgage brokers we recommend to help you get the best finance possible for your situation.

Summing up

If you take one thing away from this chapter, I hope it is this: ask lots of questions and don't take no for an answer. Real estate agents, lenders and mortgage brokers will all have different motivations. It's your job to find out as much as you can about why a bid hasn't been accepted, as well as what lenders' and brokers' preferences and policies are, and to use their answers to help you get to the next step of your investment.

CHAPTER 5

Kate begins investing

In this chapter I'm going to walk you through the step-by-step journey of what to do when you plan to buy 10 properties in 3 years. This is to give you a detailed, clear picture of exactly what happens at each step of the way. I've made up this example of Kate to illustrate it for you, but it's 100 per cent realistic and a journey I have helped many clients go on.

In this example, Kate is 31 years old, single, lives in Melbourne, has a starting deposit of $100 000 and an annual salary of $130 000. She is looking to buy these properties all on her own. She will be using my strategy of aggressive investment and the 3 golden rules. We're going to look at how she goes about:

- getting finance

- finding a broker

- knowing her borrowing capacity

- finding a property

- using a buyer's agent

- finding a conveyancer to lock in the purchase

- having the property inspected

- deciding on any dealbreakers.

How does Kate go about getting finance?

Kate has $100000 to get her going but she has big plans. She's going to need to pull equity out of her early purchases to get to her goal of 10 properties in 3 years and her financing will need to support that.

This is the first time Kate is getting finance, so she has some research to do and some decisions to make. It is okay to go directly to a bank, but because Kate is looking to buy 10 properties quickly and she hasn't taken out a mortgage before, I recommend that she speaks to a mortgage broker first.

When does Kate contact a mortgage broker?

It's best to find someone that you're happy with before you have your heart set on a property, so Kate should contact a mortgage broker *before* she has found the property she wants to buy. Having a broker in place before she's focused on a particular property means the broker can give Kate an idea of her rough borrowing capacity and what her options are. With this in mind, she then has the option of getting pre-approval if she'd like, or waiting to find the right property. (*Pre-approval* means going through a process with a bank where they assess your financial situation and on paper agree to lend you up to a certain amount of money.)

For the sake of Kate's story, I would recommend she gets pre-approval before looking seriously at the properties available on the market.

Finding a mortgage broker

If you're taking this aggressive approach to property investment, I wouldn't speak to any old broker—I'd seek out a mortgage broker who actually owns 10 or more properties themselves, so they will understand your goals and be able to point you in the right direction (chapter 4 explores why mortgage brokers may be reluctant to work with people who will be refinancing often). In Kate's case, I would recommend that she researches and interviews different brokers until she finds one that has the kind of experience and mindset to fit what she needs.

To get the process started, Kate books in a meeting with a few brokers over the phone or in person. When they talk, Kate might say, 'I read Eddie Dilleen's book, *How to Buy 10 Properties Fast*, and I want to use his strategy to do that myself. This is my current scenario. I have a full-time job and I've saved $100000 to get me going. I want to buy 10 properties in the next 3 years and I'm looking for a broker who will work with me to achieve that. I'll have to refinance along the way to pull out equity, and I know that not all brokers are up for that. Are you an investor yourself? Is this something you'd be interested in helping me with?'

Having an honest conversation like this helps you work out if a broker is interested in your investment strategy so you can narrow down which broker is going to be the best fit.

Working with a broker

When Kate decides on a mortgage broker, they will email her what is called a *broker fact find* so she can move to the next step. All mortgage broker customers need to fill in a broker fact find, which is essentially an online portal that you log into and where you can provide all the details and documentation that the broker needs so they can start looking into your loan options.

Kate's broker fact find gathers all the information her broker needs to assess her financial situation. It asks her questions about:

- what her income is
- what savings she has
- if she has any current debts
- how much superannuation she has.

Her broker has to be able to physically see what her financial situation is, so she will also be asked to upload documents to the portal as evidence, such as her pay slips and bank account statements. Her broker will need to track her savings history records and will even need to get a copy of her driver's licence and birth certificate.

Kate might feel that it's a lot of personal information to share upfront, but her broker will explain why this is necessary by saying something like, 'Buying a house is a serious financial commitment, and banks and lenders need all this information so that they feel comfortable lending to you—that's why the fact find is very in-depth.'

FYI

Mortgage brokers have certain legislation and policies that they have to work in accordance with, and registered mortgage brokers experience a high level of auditing when they are engaged to work with particular banks. If any figures turn out to be incorrect, they can get in big trouble with their licensing and a bank may even remove them from their list of brokers, so it's extremely important to give your broker everything upfront, and make sure that it is 100 per cent correct.

The broker will then analyse the information that Kate's supplied, look at her current situation and then look at the three or four main lenders that can give her the best interest rate, the best borrowing capacity and the best deals at that particular time.

Decades ago, mortgage brokers could try to push borrowers in one direction in order for them to get a higher commission from that bank, but over the last decade a lot more scrutiny and auditing has been put in place. Now, mortgage brokers legally have to show which banks are going to give buyers the best interest rate.

Kate's borrowing capacity

The broker will get back in contact with Kate to discuss her borrowing capacity. They will ask Kate how much she wants to spend and what kind of deposit she wants to use. Based on that and her $100000 in savings, her broker will likely narrow their suggestions down to three or four lenders and say something like, 'Realistically, based on your income, deposit and likely rental income, the max you could borrow at this point is probably $600000 at this particular bank for an investment loan, but your borrowing capacity at one of the third-tier lenders could be as much as $1 million.'

Different lenders offer different-sized loans based on their risk appetite, policies and interest rate offers. Some of the lenders might take into account 100 per cent of the potential rental income of Kate's investment property, while others might have a lower risk appetite and only consider 80 per cent of rental income. Chapter 4 explains the pros and cons of working with first-, second- and third-tier lenders.

So Kate's borrowing capacity depends on the lender she chooses, and her broker, like all brokers, will most likely try to gently nudge her towards the lender that will give her the best interest rate.

Then it is up to Kate to decide what size loan and with what type of interest rate she wants to take on.

Kate starts looking for her first property

At this point, Kate can start looking for a property. She's keen to start off with a smaller property in the $300 000 range, and based on her borrowing capacity getting finance should be a breeze.

To find the right property, she can either try to learn as much as possible by reading books, doing courses and then trying to find a property herself, or she can reach out to a property buyer's agent and get help finding a bargain.

Kate decides to use a buyer's agent (also called a 'buyer's advocate') because it's her first property purchase, and she works full-time. Many people use a buyer's agent for their first property purchase to help them through the experience and so they can learn along the way about how to find and negotiate great properties so they can make savvy investments on their own.

Often, new investors will buy their first one or two properties using a buyer's agent and, once they learn more, they will go off and buy future properties by themselves. As a buyer's agent myself, I've had a number of clients that have engaged me to help them buy their first three or four. They picked my brain in every conversation we had and now they are buying properties themselves.

What exactly does a buyer's agent do?

Buyer's agents can do a small part of the process or almost everything that's involved in buying a property—from finding the property and having the expertise to know it's a good buy, through to negotiating the purchase price, handling the pest and building inspections, and guiding you through to settlement. Buyer's agents often assess up to a hundred new properties each week, and then narrow it down to the ones that are unbelievable value—and these are the ones they show to their clients. They do all the due diligence, research and analysis of the property and the suburb, and then negotiate with the estate agent to bring the price down. Then, it's up to the buyer to choose whether to buy or not.

There are a number of reasons why you might consider using a buyer's agent for your investment journey. It's not essential, but it can help for the following reasons, particularly for your first few properties while you're still learning how to do it all yourself:

1. **If you're time poor.** Buying a house can be time consuming at the best of times. A buyer's agent can handle the hard work, leaving you with more time to focus on other priorities.

2. **If you want less stress.** Property hunting can be stressful, particularly in a hot market. Having someone else do most of the work means you can avoid this pressure.

3. **If you want an expert on hand.** The property sales industry is full of confusing jargon that can be tough to navigate. You can ask your agent questions about the property buying process, settlement, contracts and more.

4. **If you're unfamiliar with a city.** If you want to buy in a city or area you know nothing about, a buyer's agent can give you advice on where to buy and what kind of property to purchase to get a good rental income and capital growth in the future.

5. **If you have auction nerves.** If the idea of bidding at a property auction scares you, it might be worthwhile to

hire a buyer's agent, even if it's just for the day. Having someone else represent you means that you won't exceed your budget—you don't need to worry about adrenaline getting the better of you.

6. **If you want access to off-market properties.** Usually, working with a buyer's agent is the best way to get access to properties before they hit the market (if they do at all).

7. **If you want a better deal.** Buyer's agents are expert negotiators, so they can secure you a better price—and fast!

How does a buyer's agent get paid?

Buyer's agents are usually paid a standard flat fee or a percentage of the purchase price, depending on what they do. It can be as low as $8000, but also as high as $30000. The average is $15000. On a property worth $300000, the fee might be around $12000.

A buyer's agent will usually take a small engagement fee to start the process so they can allocate time for that specific client, which can be as little as 10 per cent. But on average it's usually a 50 per cent payment upfront and 50 per cent after the sale is done.

How fast can buyer's agents find properties?

Some agents move very quickly. A purchase could happen as soon as within one or two weeks. Of course, some clients are pickier than others. I believe it's a better investment strategy to move fast, but some clients get stuck on wanting a specific type of property. If a new client signs with me today, they could be purchasing a property (that is, signed the contract) within 10 days.

Kate needs to find a conveyancer

Back to Kate, who wants to buy in Perth. She looks at the properties that her buyer's agent has presented to her. There's a two-bedroom townhouse in Perth that she likes the look of—it's got a small parcel of land, and the floors were replaced recently. Comparable sales are around $340 000 to $360 000, and her buyer's agent has negotiated it down to $300 000.

Which means she now needs a conveyancer.

Normally, you start looking for a conveyancer when you're getting ready to buy. Since Kate is using a buyer's agent, they will be able to connect her to a conveyancer or solicitor that is registered to the same location that she wants to buy in. (You can choose your own conveyancer if you prefer them over who your buyer's agent recommends.) Kate is in Melbourne and she's buying her a property in Perth, so she would ideally use someone registered for conveyancing and soliciting in Perth.

Depending on the state you're buying in, the conveyancer can review the contracts prior to putting in an offer, or they can come into play once the offer has been accepted.

Finding your own conveyancer

A quick google will show you conveyancers and legal firms in the area you are buying in who could do the legal part of the process for you. It's always best to jump on the phone and have a quick chat about their experience to help you choose who you want to work with.

If you need help with finding the correct conveyancer, jump on my website and send an enquiry to my team. We have conveyancers we regularly use (that I use personally too), who have been working for us for the last seven years. They do conveyancing in Queensland, South Australia, New South Wales, and Western Australia. They're registered in all states around Australia, whereas many other conveyancers and solicitors can only deal in one particular state.

Contract time

Kate's buyer's agent will have negotiated the purchase price of the property for her, and she has pre-approval, so it's time to sign. Kate will have her conveyancer review the contract of sale and, if everything looks good, she will sign it subject to standard conditions of finance, pest and building inspections, which in Western Australia where she has bought is usually a 21-day condition (meaning the buyer has 21 days in which they can pull out of the contract based on one of those conditions).

Finance

The signed contract is sent to Kate's broker so they can formalise the finance, along with other information about the property such as the address and a rental appraisal. The broker will organise the bank valuation to ensure that the property valuation stacks up. (Banks do this to check you haven't bought the property for over market price, which would expose them to risk they're not willing to take.) The bank will then give Kate formal loan approval.

Time to assess the pest and building inspections

It's important the pest and building inspections happen quickly, because the reports need to be sent to the broker (who sends them to the bank) within Kate's 21-day finance period (this time period may vary, often state by state, but I almost always ask for a 21-day finance period). Kate's buyer's agent will organise the pest and building inspections to ensure they happen in good time, and the reports will usually be completed within a couple of days. Her buyer's agent will then jump on the phone and guide her through the 30–50 pages of the report, and ideally the pest and building inspectors will also give her a call to run through the details too and answer any questions.

I usually recommend that people call the pest and building inspectors themselves and chat through the report over the phone, as they will be able to explain what each section of the report means and answer any questions. This is one of the most critical parts of the process; this is where the due diligence gets done by professionals to assure you the property is a good buy. You need to know exactly what you're buying.

When Kate's buyer's agent calls her to talk through the reports, they'll likely say something like this, which I often find myself saying to my clients: 'The report is pretty long and has a lot of info. Don't freak out, take a deep breath, relax. It can be very scary the first time you look at a pest and building inspection report; it's nerve-racking reading about problems with the property you're wanting to buy. Remember that the building is 20 years old, there are bound to be a few issues or cracks here and there. These reports are created to give you information about the property, but they're often overly cautious because the pest and building inspection company needs to protect itself from any liability. The same way the bank wants to protect itself from risky borrowers, pest and building inspectors want to protect themselves from getting sued. So they often classify issues as major or minor defects and structural issues, when in reality the property is in an acceptable, normal condition for a building of its age.'

I've noticed that in these reports inspectors often classify things as major defects when it could be as simple as a couple of cracked tiles in the shower or standard building movement. Seeing 'major defect' in a report can be alarming. You have to speak to the pest and building inspector to get a more realistic picture over the phone. They often deem lots of things as 'high risk' too. I must have seen over a thousand reports over the years, and they all say high risk of potential termite activity.

When you get your inspection report back, it might seem like too many things need attention. So how do you know when something is a dealbreaker; in other words, if it will cost too much money to be worth buying the property?

The two things that can come up in these reports that tend to freak people out are termites and mould.

If your pest inspection report says they've found termites, or they think termites could be an issue, what will it cost you to rectify? If they find termites in the yard it's not a big deal—you just get the tree or fence the termites are in removed, which could cost around $2000 to $5000. If this happens you need to ask yourself if there's enough margin in the property to still make it a good deal.

It's the same with mould and moisture. If there's moisture in the walls behind shower, which is pretty common in older properties, the inspector says that it will cost up to $10 000 to fix, that's alarming. Before freaking out, call a tradie and ask for a quote. They might look at the photos in the report and say they could fix it for between $2000 and $3000. That's still not great news, but an accurate quote can be the difference between choosing to buy a property or not.

I always weigh up the cost to fix a defect against how much equity I stand to potentially make. In Kate's case, she's going to buy this property for $300 000 while other similar properties have been selling for \$340000 to \$360000. The midpoint of that is \$350000, so Kate is essentially buying this property for \$50000 under what it's worth—she's making \$50000 in equity, if not more, in purchasing it. If she has to pay \$3000 to get the shower fixed, she'll still make \$47000—which is still really good. But if it were to cost over \$10000 to fix the issues the property has, I would lean towards not going ahead with the purchase.

If Kate's worst-case scenario sees her paying \$3000 to fix the shower (which will be a tax-deductible expense), I would advise her to move forward with the purchase.

Kate decides to buy the property

Kate decides to go ahead with buying the property. Since both conditions of her contract have been satisfied, the contract of sale becomes unconditional—this is the point of no return.

Kate is issued the loan documents from her particular bank. They'll either be posted to her or sent with DocuSign to her email address. The mortgage broker will guide her from that point on to settlement, with the conveyancer's involvement too. A bank account with the bank she's chosen will be set up, and her mortgage broker will tell her to transfer the amount needed for the deposit and closing costs into that account before settlement. Settlement will likely happen two to three weeks later.

This is the time for Kate to find a good property manager, because she is about to become a landlord.

Becoming a landlord

When you become a landlord you need a property manager to look after the rental, and it's best to have someone lined up before settlement so that as soon as the property is yours no time is wasted in finding tenants. Because Kate is using a buyer's agent, they can introduce her to a good property manager in that area, who she then chooses to work with. The property manager sends her a property management form to fill in, usually by email using DocuSign, which confirms their agreement that the property manager will look after the property on Kate's behalf.

Property managers cover the day-to-day aspects of being a landlord for Kate: they find tenants, are the renter's point of contact, organise routine inspections and any maintenance needed, and they collect the rent. Kate also chooses to offload the admin of paying the council and water rates for the property to the property manager, who will pay it from the rental income. (When you are choosing an aggressive investment strategy, I always recommend outsourcing as much of the admin as you can.)

How to choose a good property manager

If you aren't using a buyer's agent, you'll need to find a good property manager on your own. I recommend first speaking with the existing property manager, as they know the property well and are hopefully good at what they do. If you aren't that impressed with them, google for property managers in that suburb. Interview them, ask how long they've been a property manager for, what their experience is and anything else you might want to know about them. Research them online and look at any reviews you can find. If you're buying in Perth, Brisbane or Adelaide, you can jump on our website (www. dilleenproperty.com.au) and make an enquiry asking for property manager recommendations.

Finding tenants

Kate's property was vacant when she bought it, so rather than keeping existing tenants she has to find people to rent it, and quickly. You want your property sitting empty for as short a time as possible—the sooner rent is coming in, the better. When vacant, the property manager will often get access to the property from the moment it goes unconditional or two weeks prior to settlement. This gives them a head start on advertising the property to find potential tenants.

They may use pre-existing photos of the property for the rental listing if the photos are relatively recent, with a disclaimer that says something like, 'These photos are as at two years ago, inspect for further information.' Otherwise, they'll organise a photographer to take photos. Then they line up inspections for prospective tenants so the tenants can move in as soon after settlement as possible.

The property manager will usually shortlist three or four really good applications, and will give you their guidance regarding who to choose. They might say, 'Look, these are my two favourites, especially this one here. This tenant has a very long track record, we've checked their references, we've checked them on all the websites to show that they don't have any red flags against a previous tenant history, so they look like the best choice.'

Kate might have her own ideas on how to choose good tenants, but I would advise her, 'You're just starting out as a landlord; I would let your experienced property manager take the lead, do their in-depth checks and guide you from there.' There are no hard and fast rules about what makes one tenant application better than another—what matters is their rental history, which your property manager will research for you.

This is why it is so important to use a property manager. Do not try to do it yourself. I have never personally managed a property—I always ask a property manager to do it for me. It's too much work; property managers have the expertise needed, and you should spend your time on other things, like growing your portfolio.

Landlord insurance

Before settlement, Kate also needs to organise building insurance and landlord insurance, which is something her buyer's agent can make recommendations about (or she can do her own research online). (Again, jump on our website www.dilleenproperty.com.au and make an enquiry for insurance recommendations.)

> **FYI**
>
> Building insurance is required by the bank *before* settlement day, so it's essential you get this done. If you are using a mortgage broker, they will remind you.

In the event that a tenant stops paying rent and abandons the property, your property manager would reach out to your landlord insurer directly and make a claim under your insurance policy. The property manager would supply your insurer with all the relevant documentation, including details on when the tenant signed the lease and how the property looked when they moved in, to add to your evidence of how much rent they owe and/ or what damage they may have done to the property if you are claiming for damage.

Landlord insurance is quite affordable; it usually costs less than $400 for the entire year, so it's good value and definitely worth it. Organising it can be done online in five to 10 minutes. I've only made two landlord insurance claims in all my time investing, and each was sorted out in about two weeks. I strongly recommend getting landlord insurance.

Settlement

Finally, settlement day arrives! On settlement day, Kate doesn't have to do anything except wait for a call. Usually her broker and/or conveyancer will call to say, 'Settlement is complete, you own this property. Congratulations!'

How much did Kate's first property cost?

Kate bought her townhouse for $300 000 and it met all 3 golden rules (buy under market value, choose properties with high rental yields, and buy in metro areas). She had the option of doing a 20 per cent, 10 per cent or 5 per cent deposit, and she chose a 5 per cent deposit with a first-tier bank. (At the time of writing, Commonwealth Bank and ANZ are offering 5 per cent investment deposit loans.)

5% deposit	$15 000
Stamp duty	$9000
Legal fees	$2000
Pest and building inspections	$1000
Bathroom moisture repairs	$3000
LMI	$10 000
Buyer's agent fee	$15 000
Total	**$55 000**

Kate was able to enter the property market for $55 000 in total, and $15 000 of that paid for her buyer's agent. If she had found the property on her own, it would have only cost her $40 000 to become a property owner.

Her tenant moves in 10 days after settlement, paying $540 a week in rent. With the purchase price of $300 000, her rental yield works out to be 9.36 per cent, which is massive.

The cashflow sheet for Kate's first property (table 5.1, overleaf) shows all her expenses, and what her cashflow will be based on an estimated lower and higher rent.

Table 5.1: cashflow for Kate's first property

Estimated expenses	Weekly	Monthly	Annually
Estimated council rates	$32.12	$139.17	$1670.00
Estimated strata fees, including building insurance	$36.54	$158.33	$1900.00
Estimated water rates (tenant pays usage)	$18.65	$80.83	$970.00
Estimated insurance	$ -	$ -	$ -
Estimated management fees	$32.69	$141.67	$1700.00
Estimated repayments 6.0% interest only, 95% loan	$328.85	$1425.00	$17 100.00
Estimated landlord Insurance	$6.92	$30.00	$360.00
Estimated totals	**$455.77**	**$1975.00**	**$23 700.00**
Income comparables			
Estimated lower rent	$500.00	$2166.67	$26 000.00
Estimated higher rent	$540.00	$2340.00	$28 080.00
Estimated cashflow before tax			
Estimated lower rent	$44.23	$191.67	$2300.00
Estimated higher rent	$84.23	$365.00	$4380.00

Summing up

Kate now owns her first property! She's feeling both exhausted and exhilarated. She's learned all about working with finance brokers and getting a mortgage with a bank, and her buyer's agent has taught her the process of buying a property, assessing pest and building inspections, and becoming a landlord. Time for property two!

CHAPTER 6
Kate buys 3 more properties

Now that Kate owns one property, she is keen to move quickly on buying more so that she can reach her goal of buying 10 properties in 3 years.

Kate starts thinking about property two

A couple of weeks after her first property settles, Kate goes back to her mortgage broker and says she's ready to buy a second property. Her broker asks to see all her financials again as her financial situation has changed through her first purchase – she now has less savings, an asset, and her cashflow has changed.

'Alright, give me all your pay slips again,' says the mortgage broker. 'Give me all your documentation again. You have a loan for the first property of $285 000, and you're getting $540 a week in rental income, which covers the loan repayments. You spent $49 000 out of $100 000, so you've got $51 000 left in savings which is enough for a deposit. You are able to buy another property already, have you thought of the type of property you want to buy?'

'I'd like to buy a property similar to the last one I bought,' replies Kate.

The broker will redo all her figures and talk to the banks, and this time they'll be taking two rental incomes into consideration—one from the property she already owns, and one from the next one she's hoping to buy.

Assuming she's going to buy another property for roughly $300 000 and it's likely to rent out for around $500 a week, she will have just over $1000 a week in combined income from rent coming in, which is $52 000 a year more than when Kate owned no property. The broker will likely come back to her to say her borrowing capacity has come down from about $600 000 (as she initially had in chapter 5 before buying her first property) to $550 000.

The more property you own—and therefore the more debt you have—the less your borrowing capacity, but Kate's hasn't come down as much as most people would anticipate because her rental yields are so much higher than what the average investor usually buys. And don't forget that while you're on the journey of buying 10 properties, you can continue saving throughout, feeding those savings into your next investments—which helps to maintain your borrowing capacity.

Buying property two

Kate asks her buyer's agent for similar properties to the first one, and a week later they send her a unit within 10 kilometres of Perth CBD that they've negotiated down to $250 000 (while other similar ones are selling for $300 000 to $310 000). It's a bargain that she doesn't want to miss out on.

The process is the same as when buying her first property. She puts down a 5 per cent deposit again.

5% deposit	$12 500
Stamp duty	$8000
Legal fees	$2000
Pest and building inspections	$1000
Lenders' mortgage insurance (LMI)	$8500
Buyer's agent fee	$15 000
Total	**$47 000**

She rents the property out for $400 a week, giving her a gross yield of 8.32 per cent.

The cashflow sheet for her second property (table 6.1, overleaf) gives you an idea of her ongoing income and expenses associated with the property.

That's property number two sorted!

Getting equity out of Kate's first two properties

Throughout her first three months of property investing, Kate has been saving $400 a week, giving her another $5000 in savings. She spent $102 000 in total buying both properties, so she now has $3000 in savings as a buffer in case something needs replacing or fixing. For the next six months, Kate keeps saving $400 a week from her income, adding another $10 000 to her savings, giving her a total of $13 000.

Table 6.1: cashflow for Kate's second property

Estimated expenses	Weekly	Monthly	Annually
Estimated council rates	$32.12	$139.17	$1670.00
Estimated strata fees, including building insurance	$42.31	$183.33	$2200.00
Estimated water rates (tenant pays usage)	$18.65	$80.83	$970.00
Estimated insurance	$ -	$ -	$ -
Estimated management fees	$32.69	$141.67	$1700.00
Estimated repayments 6.0% interest only, 90% loan	$259.62	$1125.00	$13500.00
Estimated landlord Insurance	$6.92	$30.00	$360.00
Estimated totals	**$392.31**	**$1700.00**	**$20400.00**
Income comparables			
Estimated lower rent	$400.00	$1733.33	$20800.00
Estimated higher rent	$450.00	$1950.00	$23400.00
Estimated cashflow before tax			
Estimated lower rent	$7.69	$33.33	$400.00
Estimated higher rent	$57.69	$250.00	$3000.00

By the time she reaches nine months into her first year of investing, she can consider taking equity out of her first two properties. The broker is the main person Kate needs to work with in order to achieve this—and there are a few stages to the process.

Valuations

The first step in refinancing is getting the property valued. Kate has been looking at similar properties that have sold recently in the suburb of her first property, and she is confident she can pull out a good amount of equity based on the latest sale prices.

She contacts her broker. 'I paid $300000 for my first property, and look at these similar ones now—they are selling for $330000 to $360000, and that one sold for $380000. My second property I only bought for $250000, and comparable sales are now at $310000 to $330000.'

The market doesn't need to have moved much since her purchase; she bought property one for under market value, so it's time to extract that value so she can keep investing. Her broker agrees and orders valuations from four different first-tier banks, including the banks she has her two property loans with.

The easiest way for the banks to value her properties is to do what's called a *desktop valuation*, where rather than physically inspecting each property they use data, statistics, comparable sales and market trends. The banks will then come back with their loan offers based on these desktop valuations. Each bank will give the properties a different valuation based on their internal policies.

I recommend refinancing both properties together as it's much more efficient, but to outline Kate's situation I'm going to run through the refinancing numbers for property one first.

Refinancing

On completing their desktop valuations, one bank might say Kate's first property is worth $330000, another will say $350000 and another $370000. Depending on which bank has the highest offer, Kate may have to refinance from one bank to another.

Kate's broker will talk her through the options, ranging from $330000 to $370000. Because Kate wants to take the maximum amount of equity out to buy property number three, she chooses the bank with the $370000 valuation. Taking out her equity means the loan amount for property one will be much higher and her repayments will increase, but she'll still break even on the property.

The best valuation comes from a different bank to the one she currently has her mortgage with. As her broker explains, 'We need to discharge your current mortgage to refinance, and we're going to have to do the whole finance process all over again.'

Refinancing is really just admin when you've been doing this as long as I have, but it's exciting the first time, and it helps you move on to your next purchase.

Discharging her mortgage from the first bank

Kate's new bank is going to have to take over her existing loan, paying out the old loan and issuing a new loan (in other words, *discharging the mortgage*). Kate had $285000 left on her loan, and the new bank she's refinancing with (which gave a valuation of $370000) will allow her to take the new loan up to 80 per cent or 90 per cent of that valuation price. Because Kate is taking a really aggressive approach, she chooses the 90 per cent option. Ninety per cent of $370 000 is $333 000, which becomes her new loan amount.

The equity Kate gets out is the difference between her old loan amount, $285 000, and her new loan amount of $333 000, which is $48 000.

She will need pay lenders' mortgage insurance (LMI) again of around $5000, so the total cash she receives from refinancing is $43 000.

How aggressive you want to be depends on how far you take your loan to value ratio (LVR). If Kate wanted to be conservative, she'd choose her new loan to be 80 per cent of the valuation and therefore avoid paying LMI, but that means getting less equity out—her loan amount would be $296 000, meaning she'd only get $11 000 equity out of property one.

Refinancing usually takes about four weeks, but it could be complete in as little as two weeks with a different bank, and only a week if it's with the same bank.

Kate's savings now add up to $56 000 (the $13 000 she had already plus the $43 000 of equity).

To give you an idea of how her cashflow is affected by refinancing her first property, table 6.2 (overleaf) shows the cashflow sheet for property one after refinancing.

Table 6.2: cashflow for Kate's first property after refinancing

Estimated expenses	Weekly	Monthly	Annually
Estimated council rates	$32.12	$139.17	$1670.00
Estimated strata fees, including building insurance	$36.54	$158.33	$1900.00
Estimated water rates (tenant pays usage)	$18.65	$80.83	$970.00
Estimated insurance	$ -	$ -	$ -
Estimated management fees	$32.69	$141.67	$1700.00
Estimated repayments 6.0% interest only, 90% loan	$382.69	$1658.33	$19 900.00
Estimated landlord Insurance	$6.92	$30.00	$360.00
Estimated totals	**$509.62**	**$2208.33**	**$26 500.00**
Income comparables			
Estimated lower rent	$500.00	$2166.67	$26 000.00
Estimated higher rent	$540.00	$2340.00	$28 080.00
Estimated cashflow before tax			
Estimated lower rent	−$9.62	−$41.67	−$500.00
Estimated higher rent	$30.38	$131.67	$1580.00

Refinancing her second property

Kate paid $250 000 for her second property, and she gets valuations of $300 000 and $310 000 from the four first-tier banks. She chooses the bank offering a $310 000 valuation with a 90 per cent LVR, meaning her loan amount will be 90 per cent of $310 000, which is $279 000. The difference between her existing loan amount of $225 000 and her new loan amount of $279 000 is $54 000, but she has to pay $4000 in LMI, so the total equity she pulls out of property two is $50 000.

Table 6.3 (overleaf) is the cashflow sheet of her second property after refinancing.

It's not even a year since Kate began investing and not only does she have two properties, but she has also pulled $93 000 of equity out! However, the cashflow of her second property is negatively geared after refinancing, so she starts saving more money each month to cover it. She knows she won't need to do this forever—soon the rent will go up and/or interest rates will come down a bit. Plus as she adds more cashflow-positive properties to her portfolio, they will help to even out her overall cashflow.

Her total savings have grown to $106 000! She's made way more through investing than she could ever save in a year, and she's on a good salary. Kate is pleased and ready to buy her third property.

Table 6.3: cashflow for Kate's second property after refinancing

Estimated expenses	Weekly	Monthly	Annually
Estimated council rates	$32.12	$139.17	$1670.00
Estimated strata fees, including building insurance	$42.31	$183.33	$2200.00
Estimated water rates (tenant pays usage)	$18.65	$80.83	$970.00
Estimated insurance	$ -	$ -	$ -
Estimated management fees	$32.69	$141.67	$1700.00
Estimated repayments 6.0% interest only, 90% loan	$322.12	$1395.83	$16750.00
Estimated landlord Insurance	$6.92	$30.00	$360.00
Estimated totals	**$454.81**	**$1970.83**	**$23650.00**
Income comparables			
Estimated lower rent	$400.00	$1733.33	$20800.00
Estimated higher rent	$450.00	$1950.00	$23400.00
Estimated cashflow before tax			
Estimated lower rent	−$54.81	−$237.50	−$2850.00
Estimated higher rent	−$4.81	−$20.83	−$250.00

Looking for property three

Kate is looking ahead to her next property, so she contacts her mortgage broker to get the ball rolling again. She sends him all the documentation he needs about her current financial position, and he goes to the banks and comes back to her with her borrowing capacity. She has two properties with good rental income, a good salary and a lot in savings, but her mortgages on her two properties are higher now. Her borrowing capacity ranges from $500 000 to $800 000 with different banks.

Kate feels ready to find a property herself. She has learned a lot from her buyer's agent, as well as reading books and watching YouTube videos, and she wants to find a bargain herself. With the 3 golden rules in mind, she starts looking online every day. She calls up lots of estate agents on her lunch breaks and her commute home from work, and narrows her search down to a few suburbs that she wants to try and target.

She starts the long, painful process of building up relationships with real estate agents, hoping to find something significantly under market value. She's hoping for a distressed sale, maybe something off market. Her first two properties were off market thanks to a connection her buyer's agent had with a selling agent.

She decides to call the two selling agents she bought properties one and two from. 'Hi, I'm the buyer of property X earlier in the year, and I'm after another one that's similar. I understand you're always getting new properties to look at. Do you have anything similar to the one that I bought that you're currently working on? Do you have any that aren't online yet?'

Both agents say they'll get back to her if something comes up, but a week later she hasn't heard from them and she's restless.

She refreshes real estate websites daily, filtering for the suburbs she is looking at, looking newest to oldest, and every day there are three or four new listings — but none that look promising. Though a touch disheartened, Kate is persistent.

If you don't look for two or three days, you might miss a great deal. If a property is listed at a competitive price it can sell within hours. When properties go online, you have to race everyone else to it. The more you're looking at properties, the better chance you have of beating others.

Kate keeps calling the seller's agents of properties that look alright, sharing that she's keen to buy the right thing very quickly. A few weeks later, one of the agents gets in touch with her who has three properties that aren't listed online yet, and one is a distressed sale because of a divorce. Kate asks for some photos and for the information to be emailed to her immediately. It's a duplex 30 minutes from Perth's CBD, and it looks promising. (A *duplex* is two properties on one title: dual occupancy, dual income, and very popular in Brisbane, Perth and even Adelaide, where you can still get them for $500 000 to $600 000.)

Kate jumps into action.

She does some market analysis to find out if the property is priced well at the asking price (golden rule number one). The agent said they'd be happy to sell for $525 000 for a quick sale, and comparable properties are currently listed for $540 000 to $580 000. Kate checks out similar properties that recently sold, and sees that a property very similar sold two weeks ago for $555 000, and another sold a week before that for $561 000.

Kate calls the agent back and asks how long it has been tenanted for, when it is leased until and what the tenants are like. She discovers it's been tenanted for the last three years, the current leases are until March of the following year and the current tenants have always paid their rent on time. One side is currently rented out for $400 a week, but the rent hasn't been put up in two years so it could be increased to $450 a week once the lease ends. The other side is smaller and rented for $340 a week, but that could be put up to $400 a week when the lease ends. Kate asks for a copy of the latest routine inspection report, and asks if there is any major work needed to the properties. The agent says she'll send the routine inspection reports through, and that as far as she can tell it looks in pretty good condition. It's only eight years old, so the carpets are holding up and the kitchens aren't too bad.

'If I were to put in an offer today, how long would it take for the owner to get back to you?' Kate asks, her heart thumping.

'I may be able to get hold of them today; the latest would be tomorrow morning.'

'Okay, thank you, I'll just do some final calculations and then email an offer through.'

Kate calculates what her yield would be with the current total rent on the duplex and then the increased total rent: 7.33 per cent yield, and then 8.42 per cent.

What should Kate's offer be?

When there are recent bad sales, you use those to your advantage when communicating your offer. When there are recent good sales, you don't want to mention them until the agent does because sometimes the agents don't know about them. If you're buying in a market that's very competitive and you offer $100000 less than the asking price, agents will laugh and not even consider it; it's an insult.

At $525 000 for a duplex this close to Perth it is already good value, but Kate is aiming to get it for $500 000, so she should start with an offer of $485 000. She emails it off to the agent, with the conditions of finance and pest and building inspections, and anxiously waits to hear back. Two minutes later, her phone rings.

The agent says hello with a laugh, and Kate's stomach churns with nerves. 'Can you add a bit to that offer?' the agent asks.

'The maximum I can go to is $490 000,' Kate replies.

The agent will always ask if you can go higher, even if you say no. They'll ask you for $1000 more, $3000 more, $10 000 more, depending on how aggressive the agent is.

'How about $500 000 and I'll take that to the seller,' the agent says.

Kate takes a deep breath. 'I can do a maximum of $490 000, and I can make the sale happen very quickly,' she adds.

'Okay, I'll take $490 000 to the seller, but they wanted $500 000 as a minimum,' the agent says. 'Stay near your phone, I'll call you again soon.'

Sure enough, Kate's phone rings 30 minutes later.

'Look, they really want $500 000,' the agent says, and Kate is about to say, 'Okay, let's do it' when the agent continues, 'but they'll accept $495 000 if you can settle in 30 days. That's the very lowest they'll go.'

Depending on your situation you might say, 'Unfortunately, I don't have any more money.' Or, 'I really want to buy the property, I might be able to get an extra $1000 together. I can go to $491 000.' For Kate, she's thrilled with a purchase price of $495 000 and agrees, subject to finance and pest and building inspections. She jumps off the phone and immediately emails her final offer through, and receives an email shortly after from the agent confirming the $495 000 purchase price.

Next steps

Now that her offer has been accepted, Kate has to:

- contact a conveyancer

- get the contract of sale to the conveyancer to look over

- let her mortgage broker know she's had an offer accepted

- sign the contract of sale

- get a copy of the contract of sale to her mortgage broker

- book in the pest and building inspections, giving them the selling agent's contact details so they can arrange access to the property

- pay the inspectors

- ask the selling agent for a rental appraisal (which she will send to the broker, who will send it to the bank)

- contact and arrange a property manager (because the property has existing tenants with a fixed lease, Kate chooses to keep the existing property manager).

Once Kate's finance is approved, she will also have to:

- get building and landlord insurance on the property

- have her conveyancer confirm exactly how much money needs to be in her account ready to be withdrawn at settlement

- review the pest and building inspection reports and call the inspectors to discuss their findings.

Kate is able to get a loan with a first-tier bank with a 10 per cent deposit, which she decides to do. Her mortgage broker finds her a second-tier bank that will do a 5 per cent deposit, but the interest rate is 2 per cent higher so Kate chooses to go with the first-tier bank.

How much does this duplex cost Kate to buy?

10% deposit	$49 500
Stamp duty	$18 000
Legal fees	$2000
Pest and building inspections	$1000
Lenders' mortgage insurance (LMI)	$8500
Total	**$79 000**

Table 6.4 is the cashflow sheet for her duplex to give you an idea of the weekly, monthly and yearly expenses it incurs and the income it generates.

And that's her third and fourth property added to her portfolio! Though it was only one purchase, she's bought a duplex, which is two properties on one title that bring in two rental incomes. Go Kate! Now her cashflow is much better as well; with this one purchase, she's back in the positive over her whole portfolio.

Table 6.4: cashflow for Kate's duplex (third and fourth properties)

Estimated expenses	Weekly	Monthly	Annually
Estimated council rates	$38.08	$165.00	$1980.00
Estimated strata fees, including building insurance	$ -	$ -	$ -
Estimated water rates (tenant pays usage)	$18.65	$80.83	$970.00
Estimated insurance	$23.08	$100.00	$1200.00
Estimated management fees	$36.54	$158.33	$1900.00
Estimated repayments 6.0% interest only, 90% loan	$513.46	$2225.00	$26700.00
Estimated landlord Insurance	$6.92	$30.00	$360.00
Estimated totals	**$636.73**	**$2759.17**	**$33110.00**
Income comparables			
Estimated lower rent	$700.00	$3033.33	$36400.00
Estimated higher rent	$750.00	$3250.00	$39000.00
Estimated cashflow before tax			
Estimated lower rent	$63.27	$274.17	$3290.00
Estimated higher rent	$113.27	$490.83	$5890.00

Summing up

Kate has been property investing for one year, and she owns four properties! She's learned how to find properties that meet the 3 golden rules and negotiate the purchases price all on her own. Go Kate!

Her next step is to get up to 10 properties over the next two years.

CHAPTER 7
Kate's buying spree

It's the start of year two and Kate is ready to buy more investment properties. She's hoping to buy 10 properties in 3 years, and so far she already has four properties to her name. She had $106 000 in savings, then spent $79 000 on the duplex, and she had to replace a hot water service in one of the duplex houses which cost $2000, so now she has $25 000 in savings, plus another $5000 she's saved from her income, bringing her up to $30 000.

It's too soon to pull equity out of her duplex; Kate only just bought it. She doesn't have enough in savings to buy another property, so she decides to set up a self-managed super fund (SMSF) so she can buy property with it. (I also talk about buying property with SMSFs in my book *30 Properties Before 30*.)

Using a self-managed super fund to buy property

A *self-managed super fund* (SMSF) is a super fund that you manage yourself. Rather than having your super sit with a regular super fund that manages your money for you, you make the decisions yourself about how to invest your super. You need to make sure that your SMSF meets the laws for super and taxes, and it will be audited every year, all of which your accountant will do for you. It's critical you find an accountant who is very experienced at managing SMSFs.

As investors, an SMSF is helpful because you can use it to buy property. You won't be able to take equity out of your SMSF properties to help buy future properties, but your SMSF can help you buy property today. When buying a property through an SMSF, the borrowing capacity is different to and separate from when buying property in an individual name: the SMSF owns the property, not the person. So, while personally you may have reached a point where you aren't able to buy any property for the next six or 12 months, that doesn't mean your SMSF can't.

When you buy property through an SMSF you have to pay a 20 per cent deposit, and with the loan you will need to pay principal as well as interest. The only bank I know of that will do interest only in an SMSF is Granite Financial (at the time of writing). Banks are more conservative with SMSFs, meaning the interest is usually 1 per cent higher as well.

SMSFs are usually set up with what's called a cash management account (CMA for short), and it usually takes about two months to set up. When you have an SMSF, the paperwork is trickier and you have to pay an accountant to do it for you—but the funds for that come out of your SMSF.

How difficult is it to manage an SMSF?

While you do have some initial paperwork to sign to set up your SMSF, your accountant can handle everything from there onwards. I recommend you set up automations so the rental statements are automatically sent to your accountant as well as you (your property manager can help with this), so they have what they need to prepare all the ongoing paperwork, and then you simply review and sign that paperwork.

Quiz the accountant about their SMSF experience

Ensure you work with an accountant who is experienced in setting up and managing SMSFs. Before choosing an accountant, ask them:

- How many SMSFs have you set up before?

- How long have you been setting them up for?

- How many clients on average do you work with that have bought properties through SMSFs that you set up?

- How many SMSFs do you manage roughly?

If you work with an accountant who isn't experienced at setting up and managing SMSFs they could make some grave mistakes, so make sure you choose someone who really knows what they're doing.

Kate's SMSF

Kate researches different accountants who are experienced with SMSFs, and chooses one. She has $90000 in her super account with her super fund, which is rolled over into her SMSF once set up. It costs $4000 to set up her SMSF, which comes out of her super amount, bringing it down to $86000. Kate's accountant recommends setting up her SMSF with Macquarie because it has really good reporting systems for accountants and SMSF managers. Kate agrees, and two months later it's all set up. Her super is no longer diversified in stocks or bonds and so on; it's self-managed, which means she has ultimate control over it. Kate's SMSF will be audited every year, and she (well, her accountant) will have to do an SMSF tax return too to make sure she is adhering to the relevant laws.

Kate's super payments from her employer are now automatically paid into her SMSF.

Kate reaches out to her mortgage broker to tell them she wants to buy a property through her SMSF. Her broker will assess the borrowing capacity of her SMSF based off the super contributions it receives and the likely rental income of the property she wishes to buy. Kate is on $130000 per year, her super contributions from her employer are 11 per cent (at the time of writing, the required super percentage is set to increase), which means her SMSF will receive $14300 a year ($275 per week). Banks and lenders will look at that as the key factor when assessing how much the SMSF can borrow. The property she buys will likely have a rental income of around $400 a week, which brings the SMSF's income up to $675 a week. It is the SMSF's income that lenders will use to calculate her borrowing capacity. They won't worry about her living expenses, or how much she spends on coffee or groceries every week, because the SMSF is separate to her as an individual.

SMSF property purchases must have a 20 per cent deposit; you can't opt for 5 or 10 per cent. This means she doesn't have to pay lenders' mortgage insurance (LMI), but it does require her to have a larger deposit than her previous investment properties. Kate has been buying in Perth up until now; for her next property, she decides to look for a townhouse in Adelaide for around $300000 to $350000.

She repeats the process of looking every day, getting a feel for where the market is at and the different suburb options, before narrowing her search down to a couple of suburbs in Adelaide. Then, she calls agent after agent until a good deal comes her way. She finds a townhouse that is empty and has been on the market for over a month. The owners are moving interstate and want it sold. It's listed for $350000, comparable sales are $350000 to $380000, and she is able to negotiate it down to $330000 with a 45-day settlement.

20% deposit	$66000
Stamp duty	$16000
Legal fees	$2000
Pest and building inspections	$1000
Total purchase cost	**$85000**

Table 7.1 is the cashflow sheet for Kate's SMSF property.

Table 7.1: cashflow for Kate's SMSF-financed property

Estimated expenses	Weekly	Monthly	Annually
Estimated council rates	$30.19	$130.83	$1570.00
Estimated strata fees, including building insurance	$ -	$ -	$ -
Estimated water rates (tenant pays usage)	$17.31	$75.00	$900.00
Estimated insurance	$21.15	$91.67	$1100.00
Estimated management fees	$30.77	$133.33	$1600.00
Estimated repayments 7.0% interest and principal SMSF	$403.85	$1750.00	$21000.00
Estimated landlord Insurance	$6.54	$28.33	$340.00
Estimated totals	**$509.81**	**$2209.17**	**$26510.00**
Income comparables			
Estimated lower rent	$480.00	$2080.00	$24960.00
Estimated higher rent	$500.00	$2166.67	$26000.00
Estimated cashflow before tax			
Estimated lower rent	−$29.81	−$129.17	−$1550.00
Estimated higher rent	−$9.81	−$42.50	−$510.00

Kate has now secured her fifth property, and it took $85 000, meaning she has $1000 extra in her SMSF as a buffer. Her SMSF receives $1192 a month from her employer, which will more than cover the worst-case scenario of being negatively geared by $129 each month. She's five months into year two and she has four properties in her name and one under her SMSF. She has used up her available SMSF cash, so she needs to go back to her own savings to lock in the next investment. She has $38 500 in savings ($30 000 + $8500 more saved from her income) and she hasn't released equity from properties three and four (her duplex) yet.

Time to tap into her equity again

When Kate bought the duplex for $495 000 (refer to chapter 6), the average selling price for similar properties was around $550 000 to $560 000. She put down a 10 per cent deposit for the property, making her mortgage $445 500. It has been six months since she bought it. Kate contacts her mortgage broker, and they begin the process again. Desktop valuations of the duplex come back at $560 000, $570 000 and $590 000 from first-tier banks. Because of her income, Kate has a good chance of still being able to get finance with one of the big banks, though this will likely be the last time that she'll be able to do so until her income goes up or the rents go up further down the track.

Kate takes the new loan up to a 90 per cent LVR, meaning it will be $531 000. Her existing mortgage was $445 500, meaning she has equity of $85 500 to take out. LMI costs her $9000, so she gets $76 500 out, meaning her total savings are now $115 000 (38 500 + 76 500).

(Kate could have chosen to be less aggressive and have the new loan be 80 per cent of the valuation, which would have saved her the $9000 cost of having to pay LMI, but she would have only been able to take out $26 500 of equity.)

Table 7.2 is the cashflow sheet for her duplex after refinancing, to show you how it has affected her cashflow.

Table 7.2: cashflow for Kate's duplex after refinancing

Estimated expenses	Weekly	Monthly	Annually
Estimated council rates	$38.08	$165.00	$1980.00
Estimated strata fees, including building insurance	$ -	$ -	$ -
Estimated water rates (tenant pays usage)	$18.65	$80.83	$970.00
Estimated insurance	$23.08	$100.00	$1200.00
Estimated management fees	$36.54	$158.33	$1900.00
Estimated repayments 6.0% interest only, 90% loan	$612.50	$2654.17	$31850.00
Estimated landlord Insurance	$6.92	$30.00	$360.00
Estimated totals	**$735.77**	**$3188.33**	**$38260.00**
Income comparables			
Estimated lower rent	$700.00	$3033.33	$36400.00
Estimated higher rent	$750.00	$3250.00	$39000.00
Estimated cashflow before tax			
Estimated lower rent	−$35.77	−$155.00	−$1860.00
Estimated higher rent	$14.23	$61.67	$740.00

Kate's sixth property

At six months into year two of her '10 properties in 3 years' goal (and with five properties purchased), Kate's feeling confident at finding and buying properties herself. With her $115000 in the bank, she's ready to buy property number six. She decides to diversify the location again and look in Queensland. There are townhouses available for as little as $250000 a 30–40-minute drive from the CBD, which sounds like a good next move.

She lets her mortgage broker know she's on the hunt, and dives into her property research in the new location. She reviews many different suburbs, and chats to many, many real estate agents. Colleagues at work start teasing her that she's property obsessed and never does anything else, to which she replies they should do the same! When she tells them how much equity she took from her duplex, some colleagues start asking her serious questions about property investing rather than just teasing her. It sounds too good to be true! Within a couple of weeks Kate has a clearer picture of the Brisbane market, and so she homes in on a couple of suburbs she'd like to buy in.

A week later, Kate spots a townhouse listed for $265000 that is rented out for $400 a week. At that purchase price, the gross rental yield equates to 7.84 per cent. She calls the agent and finds out the owner is buying another property and needs to sell this one to secure their finance. It hasn't had a rental increase in the last year and a half, so Kate could put the rent up to $440 in the next few months, making the gross yield 8.63 per cent. And that's before negotiating the purchase price.

She jumps on the phone and asks the agent for the most recent routine inspection report, and asks how contactable the seller is.

'I can call the seller this afternoon if you make an offer now,' the agent says.

'Okay thank you, I'll email you,' Kate replies.

Kate feels confident so she puts forward a lowball offer of $220 000. Her phone rings. Within a few minutes they land on a purchase price of $245 000, which Kate formalises over email subject to finance and building and pest inspections. She then reviews the routine inspection report and is relieved to see the townhouse looks in reasonable condition given it's 12 years old.

She calls the conveyancer she lined up the week prior to let them know, and then calls her broker.

She chooses to put down a 10 per cent deposit of $24 500 with a second-tier bank.

10% deposit	$24 500
Stamp duty	$7000
Legal fees	$2000
Pest and building inspections	$1000
Lenders' mortgage insurance (LMI)	$3500
Repairs	$2000
Total	**$40 000**

Table 7.3 (overleaf) is how the cashflow for her sixth property looks.

She now has six properties after 21 months of property investing. Her savings are at $82 000 after spending $40 000 buying property six ($75 000 plus another $7000 she has saved in the last four months).

Table 7.3: cashflow for Kate's sixth property

Estimated expenses	Weekly	Monthly	Annually
Estimated council rates	$34.23	$148.33	$1780.00
Estimated strata fees, including building insurance	$40.38	$175.00	$2100.00
Estimated water rates (tenant pays usage)	$18.65	$80.83	$970.00
Estimated insurance	$ -	$ -	$ -
Estimated management fees	$30.77	$133.33	$1600.00
Estimated repayments 6.0% interest only, 90% loan	$253.85	$1100.00	$13 200.00
Estimated landlord Insurance	$6.92	$30.00	$360.00
Estimated totals	**$384.81**	**$1667.50**	**$20 010.00**
Income comparables			
Estimated lower rent	$400.00	$1733.33	$20 800.00
Estimated higher rent	$440.00	$1906.67	$22 880.00
Estimated cashflow before tax			
Estimated lower rent	$15.19	$65.83	$790.00
Estimated higher rent	$55.19	$239.17	$2870.00

Properties seven and eight

With six properties secured, Kate is feeling great. She has been able to increase the rent on her first three properties, which improves her cashflow, and she's ready to buy another property. She loved the efficiency of buying two properties in one with her duplex, and decides to look for another. She looks in Perth again and finds a duplex for $550000. It was listed for $580000 but she negotiates them down. (Comparable sales are $600000, so Kate feels confident she's bought under market value.)

Kate has to do a 5 per cent deposit with a third-tier lender, which is her first time using a lender like this. She feels a little nervous, but her broker reassures her that they're established and reputable. With her savings of $82000 she doesn't have enough money to pay a 10 per cent deposit plus stamp duty and LMI, so she has no choice. She considers pulling out and buying a smaller property instead, but she really likes this duplex so she decides to go ahead. The two properties are rented for $770 a week combined, which gives a gross rental yield of 7.28 per cent.

5% deposit	$27500
Stamp duty	$20000
Legal fees	$2000
Pest and building inspections	$1000
Lenders' mortgage insurance (LMI)	$30000
Total purchase cost	**$80500**

Table 7.4 (overleaf) is the cashflow sheet for her duplex. As you can see, it is going to cost her a few thousand dollars every year, until the rents go up or interest rates come down.

Table 7.4: cashflow for this property

Estimated expenses	Weekly	Monthly	Annually
Estimated council rates	$42.31	$183.33	$2200.00
Estimated strata fees, including building insurance	$ -	$ -	$ -
Estimated water rates (tenant pays usage)	$27.31	$118.33	$1420.00
Estimated insurance	$23.08	$100.00	$1200.00
Estimated management fees	$48.08	$208.33	$2500.00
Estimated repayments 7.0% interest only, 95% loan	$701.92	$3041.67	$36 500.00
Estimated landlord Insurance	$6.92	$30.00	$360.00
Estimated totals	**$849.62**	**$3681.67**	**$44 180.00**
Income comparables			
Estimated lower rent	$770.00	$3336.67	$40 040.00
Estimated higher rent	$820.00	$3553.33	$42 640.00
Estimated cashflow before tax			
Estimated lower rent	−$79.62	−$345.00	−$4140.00
Estimated higher rent	−$29.62	−$128.33	−$1540.00

Kate only has $1500 left of her savings, which is cutting it fine. She feels nervous that if something were to break at one of her properties, she might not have enough money to fix it, so she decides to be extra frugal and save more of her income than usual. She wonders if she should have bought a smaller property rather than the second duplex, but what's done is done.

By the end of year two she has eight properties, and thanks to her saving efforts she has $8000 in savings, helping her sleep a little easier at night. She was able to increase the rent on the new duplex to a combined $800 a week, leaving the property $2500 in the red each year. She knows that as soon as she can bring the interest rate down on the loan the property will become neutrally geared; alternatively, once she buys another smaller property with a better yield, it will even her portfolio out.

Refinancing to lock in her final two properties

Kate has a break from buying property for the first three months of year three. She wants to give property six a bit more time to appreciate in value before she refinances, so she saves as much as she can from her income. By the end of March she has $15000 in savings, and she contacts her broker to begin refinancing property six—the one she bought in Queensland for $245000. At the time she bought it, comparable properties were selling for around $300000, and it's had nine months of appreciation since then, so she's confident the desktop valuations will come back strong.

Her broker contacts her to share that one bank valued it at $300000, another at $320000, and another at $340000. She chooses to refinance with the bank that gave her the highest valuation of $340000.

Because she put down a 10 per cent deposit on the Queensland property, her loan was only $220500. She decides to be more conservative this time and takes the new loan up to 80 per cent, avoiding LMI. This means her new loan is $272000, giving her $51500 of equity. This brings her total savings up to $66500.

Properties nine and ten for Kate

Kate chooses a very affordable property for purchase number nine. She picks up a very cheap one-bedroom unit in Perth for $180000 (which you can still get today, believe it or not). Here's how much it costs her.

10% deposit	$18000
Stamp duty	$4500
Legal fees	$2000
Pest and building inspections	$1000
Lenders' mortgage insurance (LMI)	$2500
Total	**$30000**

Her one-bedroom unit in Perth is rented for $360 per week, giving her a 10.4 per cent gross yield. Table 7.5 is the cashflow sheet for this property, which helps even out the cashflow of her portfolio, given that her second duplex (properties 7 and 8) has negative cashflow.

Table 7.5: cashflow for Kate's ninth property

Estimated expenses	Weekly	Monthly	Annually
Estimated council rates	$31.54	$136.67	$1640.00
Estimated strata fees, including building insurance	$53.85	$233.33	$2800.00
Estimated water rates (tenant pays usage)	$18.65	$80.83	$970.00
Estimated insurance	$ –	$ –	$ –
Estimated management fees	$28.85	$125.00	$1500.00
Estimated repayments 6.0% interest only, 90% loan	$187.12	$810.83	$9730.00
Estimated landlord Insurance	$6.92	$30.00	$360.00
Estimated totals	**$326.92**	**$1416.67**	**$17 000.00**
Income comparables			
Estimated lower rent	$360.00	$1560.00	$18 720.00
Estimated higher rent	$400.00	$1733.33	$20 800.00
Estimated cashflow before tax			
Estimated lower rent	$33.08	$143.33	$1720.00
Estimated higher rent	$73.08	$316.67	$3800.00

Kate saves another $4500 while property nine settles, which brings her savings to $41 000. She gets straight on with looking for property 10.

She finds a two-bedroom unit in Adelaide for $200 000, well under market value, with comparable properties selling for $245 000 to $250 000. The small front garden is completely overgrown, so she budgets to spend $500 on a gardener to make it presentable. She only has $41 000 in savings so the maximum deposit she can do is 10 per cent, but the bank tells her she has to do a 20 per cent deposit. She goes back to her broker, and ends up choosing a third-tier bank who will accept her 10 per cent deposit.

10% deposit	$20 000
Stamp duty	$8500
Legal fees	$2000
Pest and building inspections	$1000
Lenders' mortgage insurance (LMI)	$2500
Total	**$34 000**

The property is already rented out for $330 per week, giving her a gross rental yield of 8.58 per cent. She will be able to increase the rent to at least $350 per week once the lease is up, possibly as high as $370 per week. This cashflow sheet (table 7.6) shows how this property will affect her cashflow when it's rented out for $330 or $370 a week.

Table 7.6: cashflow for Kate's tenth property

Estimated expenses	Weekly	Monthly	Annually
Estimated council rates	$30.58	$132.50	$1590.00
Estimated strata fees, including building insurance	$34.62	$150.00	$1800.00
Estimated water rates	$17.69	$76.67	$920.00
Estimated insurance	$ -	$ -	$ -
Estimated management fees	$30.77	$133.33	$1600.00
Estimated repayments 6.0% interest only	$207.69	$900.00	$10 800.00
Estimated landlord Insurance	$6.73	$29.17	$350.00
Estimated totals	**$328.08**	**$1421.67**	**$17 060.00**
Income comparables			
Estimated lower rent	$330.00	$1430.00	$17 160.00
Estimated higher rent	$370.00	$1603.33	$19 240.00
Estimated cashflow before tax			
Estimated lower rent	$1.92	$8.33	$100.00
Estimated higher rent	$41.92	$181.67	$2180.00

Summing up

Kate has met her goal of buying 10 properties in 3 years and can still take equity out of properties seven, eight, nine and 10. She's got her own SMSF, through which she can keep buying properties as the years go by. Plus, she still has $7000 in savings. I would predict that she will keep buying investment properties.

People get hooked doing this. You've got ups and downs, peaks and troughs. Sometimes things break and you've got to spend $5000 on this, $2000 on that, but as you can see, if you're doing a repeatable process like this, you can get into the market fairly easily and continue investing if you follow the 3 golden rules. Some people keep going; it becomes like a real-life Monopoly game.

Kate has bought 10 properties in 3 years, but this time frame may not suit everyone. In the next two chapters I look at two different scenarios — buying 10 properties in 1 year and buying 10 properties in 7 years.

CHAPTER 8

Angela and David buy 10 properties in 1 year

Some people want to buy properties fast, so let's run through the made-up example of Angela and David, who decide they want to buy 10 properties in 1 year. Just like Kate, I have developed their investment journey based off countless clients I have worked with who have done exactly this. Let's dive in.

Angela (41) and David (45) have a collective family income of $300000 a year. Angela is a full-time nurse on $100000, and her husband runs his own small business making $200000 a year. They have owned and lived in their house in the eastern suburbs of Melbourne for over a decade. It's worth $1.5 million, and their mortgage is $500000. They are going to refinance their home to meet their investment goal.

Refinancing their mortgage

To be super-aggressive in their mission to buy 10 properties in one year, Angela and David take $700000 of equity out of their home as a side loan, which brings their total loan amount to $1.2 million. Because of their combined annual income, they can afford the increase in repayments. It will mean they can't save much because their income will all be going into their mortgage repayments, but $700000 is enough to buy 10 properties so they won't need to save any more.

Angela and David put the $700000 in an offset account against their home loan so it's saving them interest until they need to use it. Now, it's time for them to go on a house-buying spree.

Buy, buy, buy

Angela and David use a buyer's agent to find properties that fit the 3 golden rules—they don't want to spend the time researching and finding properties themselves. Their buyer's agent has a few properties available that tick all their boxes, and they choose a townhouse in Perth for $350000, where comparable properties are selling for just under $400000. It's currently rented out for $480 a week (giving it a 7.13 per cent gross yield), but the rent could be increased to $550 a week when the lease ends in three months' time (making the gross yield 8.17 per cent).

Their mortgage broker finds them the best deal with a first-tier bank, and they opt for a 5 per cent deposit of $17500. With stamp duty, legal fees, the pest and building inspections, lenders' mortgage insurance (LMI) and the buyer's agent fee, their first investment property costs them $60000 (less than 10 per cent of the $700000 they have available for investments).

5% deposit	$17500
Stamp duty	$11000
Legal fees	$2000
Pest and building inspections	$1000
Lenders' mortgage insurance (LMI)	$13500
Buyer's agent fee	$15000
Total	**$60000**

Buyer's agents fees usually range from $10000 to $30000 per property, with $15000 being most common, which is why we're using $15000 in these examples. But if a property has a lesser purchase price, for example under $280000, the fee is usually $10000. And for purchase prices over $600000, the fee is usually around $20000.

FYI

It's only two weeks into the year and they have a signed contract of sale, with settlement scheduled for a month's time.

Angela and David tell their buyer's agent they're ready for property number two, and a week later they choose to buy a $600000 duplex in Perth. Comparable properties are selling for $660000 at the time of purchase, so they're thrilled. The combined rental income from both properties comes to $830 per week, which works out to be a yield of 7.19 per cent.

Their mortgage broker gets them a good interest rate for a different first-tier bank, and they go with a 10 per cent deposit.

	10% deposit	$60 000
	Stamp duty	$23 000
	Legal fees	$2000
	Pest and building inspections	$1000
	Lenders' mortgage insurance (LMI)	$10 000
	Buyer's agent fee	$15 000
	Total	**$111 000**

Purchasing this $600 000 property using a buyer's agent cost them a total of $111 000, including the $15 000 agent's fee.

Before this property is settled, Angela goes online and finds a unit listed for $240 000 in Perth — with no buyer's agent involvement. She can see it has some access issues, and over a few stressful days she is able to negotiate it down to $218 000. Comparable properties are selling for $260 000 at the time. It's rented for $350 a week, giving it an 8.35 per cent yield. The current tenants have been there for over a year, and their lease has 10 months left on it.

Some people think they have to wait for properties to settle before a bank will give them another loan, but this isn't the case. I've seen people buy four properties at once. Angela and David's mortgage broker gets them a loan with a first-tier bank accepting a 10 per cent deposit.

	10% deposit	$21 800
	Stamp duty	$6000
	Legal fees	$2000
	Pest and building inspections	$1000
	Lenders' mortgage insurance (LMI)	$3000
	New carpet	$3200
	Total	**$37 000**

They are now two months into the year, and they have signed the contracts for four investment properties. They have spent $208 000 to buy them all, which means they still have $492 000 available to buy more properties.

Two-and-a-half months into the year, their buyer's agent calls them with another property. It's in Brisbane, the sale price is $350 000 and comparable properties are selling for $400 000 to $420 000. It's currently rented for $430 a week, giving it a 6.39 per cent yield. (The rental yields in Brisbane are a little lower than Perth and Adelaide at the time of writing.)

They opt for a 5 per cent deposit while they are still able to get one.

5% deposit	$17 500
Stamp duty	$12 000
Legal fees	$2000
Pest and building inspections	$1000
Lenders' mortgage insurance (LMI)	$13 500
Buyer's agent fee	$15 000
Shower screen replaced	$1000
Total	**$62 000**

They're now three months into the year and the first three properties have settled, the fourth is about to settle and they've just signed a contract of sale for the fifth property. They go on holiday to Europe for six weeks (they were meant to go on this holiday in 2020 but the COVID-19 pandemic delayed it).

When they come back from Europe, all their properties have settled, so Angela starts hunting online again while David focuses on his business. Then her buyer's agent calls with two properties available in the same complex in Perth for $288000 each. These properties are valued between $340000 and $370000, but they are heavily discounted because the buyer's agent is organising the purchase of eight units at once. Angela and David do some rental analysis and find out they could rent each unit for $450 a week because the units are only a year old. They quickly decide to go for it.

Their mortgage broker lets them know that the first-tier banks want 20 per cent deposits, but a second-tier bank is willing to do 10 per cent deposits with a comparable interest rate, so they go for it.

The figures for each of these two properties are the same, as shown in the following grid. The only difference is that their buyer's agent gives them a 50 per cent discount for the buyer's agent fee for the second property because they are buying two at once, so they are able to secure both properties for a total of $111500, with a 30-day settlement.

10% deposit	$28800	$28800
Stamp duty	$9000	$9000
Legal fees	$2000	$2000
Pest and building inspections	$1000	$1000
Lenders' mortgage insurance (LMI)	$3700	$3700
Buyer's agent fee	$15000	$7500
Total	**$59500**	**$52000**

Angela and David manage to rent both properties out within 10 days thanks to the desirable location.

They are now six months into the year and they have already settled on seven properties. In total, Angela and David have spent $381500 on property. They still have $318500 left of their savings.

At this stage, Angela wants to diversify and buy a freestanding house. She finds a house in Perth for $400000, with comparable properties selling for $430000. It's the traditional three-bedroom two-bathroom house that everybody wants for an investment. The house is rented for $460 a week, giving it a low yield of 5.98 per cent.

Their mortgage broker contacts numerous lenders, and they choose to do a 20 per cent deposit with a first-tier lender.

In general, the larger the deposit, the lower the interest rate, so some people choose to provide bigger deposits when they want to focus on getting lower interest rates.

FYI

20% deposit	$80000
Stamp duty	$13000
Legal fees	$2000
Pest and building inspections	$1000
Total	**$96000**

It's eight months into the year and the air-conditioning unit in one of their duplex properties needs to be replaced, costing them $3000. They have $219500 left, and two more properties to buy.

Their buyer's agent finds a two-bedroom townhouse in Perth for $340000. Comparable sales are $380000 to $400000, and it's currently rented out for $500 a week, giving a gross yield of 7.65 per cent. The rent could be increased to $550 when the lease ends, making the gross yield 8.41 per cent. Though Angela enjoyed buying a standalone house, it's clear smaller properties have better yields.

20% deposit	$68 000
Stamp duty	$11 000
Legal fees	$2000
Pest and building inspections	$1000
Buyer's agent fee	$15 000
Total	**$97 000**

Angela and David have $122 500 left and are looking for property number 10. Angela scours real estate websites for a few weeks but nothing promising comes up.

Ten months into the year, their buyer's agent contacts them with a three-bedroom house for $450 000 in Perth. Comparable sales are between $490 000 and $510 000, and the rent is $570 a week, giving it a yield of 6.59 per cent. However, comparable rental properties are charging $610 a week, which would increase the gross yield to 7.05 per cent. They decide to go ahead. Their broker is able to get them a 10 per cent loan with a second-tier bank.

10% deposit	$45 000
Stamp duty	$16 000
Legal fees	$2000
Pest and building inspections	$1000
Lenders' mortgage insurance (LMI)	$7000
Buyer's agent fee	$15 000
Total	**$86 000**

Summing up

Angela and David have made it to the end of the year. They own 10 properties and haven't taken equity from any of them. They have $36 500 left in savings as a buffer, which they decide to leave in their offset account for the house they're living in so they have cash in reserve in case it's needed. They bought their properties for well under market value, making between $30 000 and $60 000 on each purchase compared to comparable sales, giving them $410 000 of equity sitting across their portfolio. They haven't even had to set up a self-managed super fund (SMSF) to reach 10 properties in one year. If Angela and David want to continue investing to get to 15 or 20 properties, they could set up an SMSF and buy a few through there, and they could also refinance their first properties to get out equity.

Some of my clients who are very much like Angela and David get hooked and want to keep buying more properties; others want to focus on paying down their mortgage or going on an overseas holiday. Regardless, they're in the market and their properties are working for them.

CHAPTER 9

Anthony buys 10 properties in 7 years

When I started investing, I was on a measly salary with no assets to my name—so I totally understand that not everyone has the income Kate does, or the assets and incomes that Angela and David do to get the same head start with property investing. But although I work with many clients on big salaries, I also have plenty who earn between $50 000 and $70 000 a year.

In this final made-up example, I follow the investment journey of Anthony, who wants to purchase 10 properties in 7 years. He is 22, living in a shared house in Sydney, and he earns $65 000 a year in the customer service industry. Anthony has $25 000 in savings, which is awesome, but it's not quite enough to buy yet. So his story starts with him working and saving so he can start his property-buying journey. His take-home pay is $1000 a week, of which he saves $200 a week.

Anthony buys his first property

Six months after deciding he wants to invest in property, he has $30 000 in savings. He's spent the last six months reading multiple property investment books, watching YouTube videos, learning all he can. He even invests $500 into a course on property investment (giving him $29 500 left to buy his first property).

> **FYI**
>
> Anthony doesn't have enough savings to pay for a buyer's agent to help him, so he will look for every investment property himself. He's done the research, learned all he can about whose help he will need at each stage (mortgage brokers, pest and building inspectors, conveyancers), and he is taking action himself. You can too. I didn't use a buyer's agent to get started; I learned all I could from books and other resources, and got cracking.

Anthony scours online listings, looking every day. Eventually he sees a one-bedroom unit in Perth for $220 000 that looks promising. It was originally listed for $230 000, and he manages to negotiate it down to $200 000. There are similar units on the market for $230 000 to $250 000.

Anthony uses the mortgage broker his uncle recommended, and decides to do a 5 per cent deposit with a first-tier bank. He uses a conveyancer he found online who charges less than solicitors do. (When I was starting out, I only used conveyancers.)

5% deposit	$10 000
Stamp duty	$5500
Legal fees	$1000
Pest and building inspections	$1000
Lenders' mortgage insurance (LMI)	$6000
Total	**$23 500**

He's amazed it costs him less than $25 000 to buy his first property! He rents it out for $370 a week, giving him a gross yield of 9.62 per cent.

Refinancing for property two

Anthony has $6000 left of his savings, and for the next six months he continues working and saving. At the end of the year he has $11 000 in savings and he's ready to refinance his first property.

He contacts his mortgage broker, who gets the ball rolling. The highest valuation comes back from a different first-tier lender, who values his unit at $260 000. They will allow him to refinance it up to 90 per cent, so his new loan will be $234 000.

Anthony's original loan was $190 000, giving him $44 000 to extract, minus $4000 of lenders' mortgage insurance (LMI), meaning he has $40 000 deposited into his account. This gives him a total of $51 000 to buy his next property.

He looks in Perth again. He was very happy with his previous experience there, and after a few weeks he finds out about an off-market two-bedroom unit. The sellers want $275 000 for it, but he's able to negotiate it down to $250 000 because he can get the deal done quickly.

Anthony puts down a 5 per cent deposit on this property with the same first-tier lender. Because of his full-time income and the low purchase price, they are happy to give him a 95 per cent loan. He arranges to have the LMI fee of $7500 added to the loan amount, so he doesn't have to pay as much upfront. (This makes his loan $245 000 after deducting the deposit and adding the LMI fee to the loan.)

5% deposit	$12 500
Stamp duty	$7500
Legal fees	$1000
Pest and building inspections	$1000
Total	**$22 000**

It is already tenanted for $350 a week, but comparable rents are $400 a week so he knows the yield will increase as soon as the lease ends in four months' time.

Looking for a bigger property

Anthony has $29 000 in savings left and is keen to buy another property. He gets a call from the property manager of his first property who says that the carpet needs to be replaced, which costs $1000. His savings are down to $28 000. He continues saving every week, and one and a half years into this journey he has $33 000 in savings. He decides to continue saving for another three months (bringing his savings to $35 500) and then refinance his second property so he can buy something bigger.

He contacts his broker, who begins getting desktop valuations for property number two. The highest valuation comes back at $330 000, and his loan on the property is $245 000. He takes this property up to a 90 per cent loan to value ratio (LVR), which makes the new loan amount $297 000. He also has to pay $7000 LMI, giving him $45 000 of equity.

Anthony now has $80 500 in his account to buy his third property.

He's been looking at houses around Adelaide and Perth for the past three months, calling agents and sussing out different suburbs. He comes across a house 40 minutes from Adelaide that looks promising.

The asking price is $440000, and over a couple of days of negotiations he brings it down to $400000. Based on other comparable sales he thinks the house is worth up to $460000, so he's thrilled. He agrees a 5 per cent deposit with a second-tier bank.

5% deposit	$20000
Stamp duty	$20000
Legal fees	$1000
Pest and building inspections	$1000
Lenders' mortgage insurance (LMI)	$15000
Total	**$57000**

The house rents for $560 a week, giving him a gross yield of 7.28 per cent.

It's the end of his second year when the property settles, and he still has $23500 left plus a further $2500 he's saved from his income. Then the air-con unit in his second property breaks and it costs him $2000 to replace, which he finds really frustrating. His savings are now at $24000.

New opportunities in year three

Anthony gets a promotion at work, increasing his salary to $70000 a year. He decides to move into a nicer shared house that costs a bit more, and he continues saving $200 a week. He works and saves for the next six months, bringing his savings up to $29000.

It's been six months since his third property settled, and it's time to get his equity out. He contacts his broker and a week later hears fantastic news – a second-tier bank has valued the property at $520000 as the area has boomed since he bought it. He's over the moon.

Anthony refinances with this bank and chooses to make the loan 90 per cent of the valuation, making his new loan amount $468000. He has to pay $18000 in LMI, but because his old loan was $380000, he still gets a whopping $70000 deposited into his account. His total savings now add up to $99000.

Anthony dives back into looking at properties online, utilising his lunch breaks to call agents. After a few weeks, an agent calls him back to let him know they have an off-market opportunity he may be interested in. It's a unit close to Perth's CBD with two bedrooms and one bathroom, overlooking a park. The owner wants to sell quickly due to divorce and is open to offers of around $320000. Anthony negotiates back and forth, and the next day the purchase price of $300000 is agreed upon. A similar unit a block away sold for $345000 two weeks ago, so Anthony feels confident it's a good deal. The bathroom vanity needs to be replaced, which will cost $1000, but the kitchen has been renovated recently.

His broker is able to organise a 5 per cent deposit with a second-tier bank, which he chooses to go for.

5% deposit	$15000
Stamp duty	$9000
Legal fees	$1000
Pest and building inspections	$1000
Lenders' mortgage insurance (LMI)	$9000
New vanity	$1000
Total	**$36000**

Anthony rents the unit out for $420 a week, giving him a gross yield of 7.28 per cent. He now has $63000 in savings.

A week after signing the contract of sale for his fourth property, he sees a townhouse 30 minutes from Adelaide advertised for offers over $330 000. He's interested and calls the agent. The agent says they won't accept offers lower than that, so he moves on and looks for other options. Two weeks later he sees a price reduction in the listing of the townhouse: 'offers over $310 000 considered'. He looks up recent comparable sales, but there aren't many townhouses in this suburb that have sold recently. The last one sold four months ago for $333 000.

Anthony calls the agent, and finds out the owner is motivated to sell. He puts in an offer for $290 000, which is instantly rejected by the agent, so he asks the agent to chat to the seller and come back to him with a counteroffer. Two hours later he gets a call: the lowest they'll go is $305 000. Anthony says he'll think about it. Two days later he emails through his 'best and final offer of $298 000 with a 30-day settlement, subject to finance, pest and building inspections'. It's accepted!

He does a 10 per cent deposit of $29 800 with a first-tier bank.

10% deposit	$29 800
Stamp duty	$14 200
Legal fees	$1000
Pest and building inspections	$1000
Lenders' mortgage insurance (LMI)	$4000
Total	**$50 000**

Anthony is able to rent it out for $440 a week, giving him a yield of 7.67 per cent. He has $13 000 savings left.

Buying a property to live in

By the end of year three, Anthony's savings have increased to $18 000, and he decides that he wants to buy a property of his own to live in next. He'll have to refinance his fourth and fifth investment properties to afford it. He starts looking for what's available within a 40-minute commute of Sydney, and feels disheartened by how much they cost. He considers living a bit further from the city so he can get something more affordable.

Three months into year four he begins refinancing. It's been six months since he bought his last two properties, and the highest desktop valuations come back at $360 000 each.

His fourth property has a mortgage of $285 000. He takes the new loan to 90 per cent LVR, making it $324 000. He has to pay LMI of $4000, and he gets $35 000 out.

His fifth property has a mortgage of $268 200, and the new loan (again 90 per cent LVR) is $324 000. After paying LMI of $5000, he has $50 800 deposited into his account. His savings, which were at $20 500 (he saved an additional $2500 over those first three months of the year), grow to $106 300 with the equity from both of the refinanced properties.

Anthony is on the hunt for his own place to live. He goes to inspections every weekend for a couple of months, and eventually finds a nice two-bedroom, one-bathroom unit for $450 000.

His broker gets to work, and a first-tier bank is happy for him to do a 5 per cent deposit because it's a property he intends to live in.

5% deposit	$22 500
Stamp duty	$15 000
Legal fees	$1000
Pest and building inspections	$1000
Lenders' mortgage insurance (LMI)	$17 000
Total	**$56 500**

With the mortgage repayments, he will no longer be able to save money each week. The property settles a month later, and he spends $1000 on a removalist and another $5800 on furniture and white goods to set it up. A friend of his moves into the spare bedroom, paying $200 a week in rent, which helps him afford the repayments. This is the sixth property Anthony buys, and he has $43000 left in savings.

Buying properties seven and eight in year five

By the end of year four, Anthony has settled into his new home and he starts thinking about property number seven.

Anthony looks for properties in Brisbane, and finds a three-bedroom, one bathroom, one-car unit in the Logan council, which is a 30-minute drive from Brisbane CBD. It's listed for $250000, but he is able to negotiate it down to $228000 because it's currently tenanted, which has made it hard to sell. The tenant has been in there for seven years and is currently paying $350 a week in rent, and is on a fixed lease for another 10 months. When the lease is up, Anthony can easily raise the rent to $400 a week. Comparable properties are on the market for $270000, so he's thrilled with the purchase price.

Anthony does a 10 per cent deposit with a second-tier lender.

10% deposit	$22800
Stamp duty	$7200
Legal fees	$1000
Pest and building inspections	$1000
Lenders' mortgage insurance (LMI)	$3000
Total	**$35000**

With the rent at $350 a week, his gross yield is 7.98 per cent, and in 10 months' time his yield will increase to 9.12 per cent.

Anthony's story spans seven years, and of course the investment landscape will change over that time. Where to buy, and the kind of property you buy following the 3 golden rules, changes as time goes on. A few years ago you could buy houses for under $300000 in Ipswich in Brisbane, which are now worth over $500000. But this doesn't mean you've missed the boat. As prices go up, you can still find affordable properties, it's just that the type of property changes. Those were three-bedroom houses, and now to get a property for under $300000 you might need to get a one- or two-bedroom unit. Or you might buy a two-bedroom townhouse rather than a four-bedroom house. There are always suburbs worth buying in, and always properties to buy. I've been using the same strategy for over a decade; it works over time.

It's three months into year five and a now 27-year-old Anthony owns seven properties and has $8000 in savings. He waits six months and then refinances property seven so he can buy another property.

Property seven is valued at $280000. He is able to take the new loan to a 90 per cent LVR, making it $252000. His old loan is $205200, LMI costs him $2800, which gives him $44000 deposited into his account. He now has $52000 of savings.

Anthony looks for another affordable property in Brisbane, Perth and Adelaide, and ends up choosing a one-bedroom, one-bathroom unit in Perth that's listed for $220000. He negotiates back and forth with the agent, and gets the property for $200000. It's got a tenant on a fixed lease for another three months paying $320 a week, giving him a gross yield of 8.32 per cent. Comparable properties have recently sold between $245000 and $250000, so he's pleased with the purchase price.

He is able to do a 10 per cent deposit with a third-tier lender.

10% deposit	$20 000
Stamp duty	$5500
Legal fees	$1000
Pest and building inspections	$1000
Lenders' mortgage insurance (LMI)	$2500
Total	**$30 000**

Anthony now has $22 000 in savings, and eight properties, at the end of year five.

The rental yield from Anthony's first five properties will have gone up over the years, covering the increase in mortgage repayments from refinancing the properties. The goal is to have the cashflow of your property portfolio be neutral to positive. Sometimes you may have one property that is slightly negative in cashflow, but as long as the others have a positive cashflow to cover it, you'll be fine. Managing your cashflow is a critical part of being a property investor.

FYI

Changing focus in year six

Anthony ends up taking six months off property investing. He has started a new relationship, which happily distracts him, and he's pleased with his eight properties and his progress so far. Halfway through year six he decides it's time to refocus, and he chooses to set up an SMSF to buy property nine. He's been watching my YouTube videos since the start of his investment journey, and he inquires through my website asking for a referral to an account with specialised experience in SMSFs.

Anthony has been working since he was 15, and he has $65000 in super. It costs $4000 to set up his SMSF, which brings his super amount down to $61000. He contacts his broker, who organises pre-approval for him, and then he starts looking for a property. He's hoping to buy something for around $200000 because he'll need to do a 20 per cent deposit (all SMSF properties require a $20 per cent deposit), but he can't find anything promising. He contacts some agents that he's bought from in the past, and eventually an agent from a few years ago comes back to him with an off-market opportunity. It's a two-bedroom unit 30 minutes from Adelaide that's from a deceased estate. It has a tenant on a six-month lease for $360 a week, and they just want to sell it. Comparable sales are around $280000, and with much back and forth, Anthony is able to negotiate it down to $220000. The gross yield is 8.5 per cent. The building inspector lets him know the air-con unit is broken, so he will have to pay $2000 for a new one.

20% deposit	$44000
Stamp duty	$10000
Legal fees	$1000
Pest and building inspections	$1000
New AC unit	$2000
Total	**$58000**

By the end of year six, property nine is locked down and he has $3000 left in his SMSF as a buffer.

Refinancing property one again

At the start of year seven, Anthony contacts his broker to begin refinancing his eighth property, but his broker comes back to him recommending he refinance property one again. It's been nearly six years since he bought it, and his broker has had it valued at $400000. His existing loan is $234000, and he can only take the new loan up to 80 per cent LVR, making the new loan $320000. This gives him $86000 plus his $22000 of savings, a total of $108000.

Anthony starts looking for properties. The Olympics is coming to Brisbane in 2032, so he decides to buy there. After a month of looking and calling agents, he finds a two-bedroom, one-bathroom unit listed for $375000 that is currently tenanted, with comparable properties selling for around $400000. He starts negotiating, and eventually they agree on $350000. He has to do a 20 per cent deposit and is able to get a loan with a first-tier bank, but there is no LMI.

20% deposit	$70000
Stamp duty	$12000
Legal fees	$1000
Pest and building inspections	$1000
Total	**$84000**

It's rented out for $500 a week, giving him a yield of 7.42 per cent.

Anthony is 30 years old and he has bought 10 investment properties within 7 years. His relationship is getting serious, so they're keen to buy a better property to live in together. He still has $24000 in savings, and he's planning to refinance his second investment property again to finance the deposit for the property they'll buy together. His portfolio is ticking along well, with the rent he receives paying for the mortgage repayments and all outgoing expenses. He's so glad he dedicated himself to property investment; even though he doesn't have a big salary, he's been able to set himself up financially. When he's 60, all the properties will be mortgage free, giving him an incredible retirement. Figure 9.1 (overleaf) shows how his portfolio is likely to grow over the next 30 years.

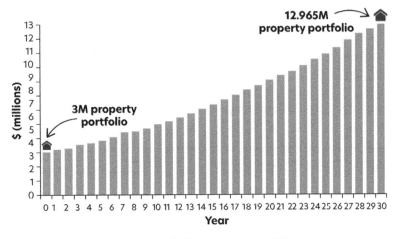

Figure 9.1: a $3 million portfolio growing at 6% per year

He'll end up being able to retire younger than his peers if he wants to, and I have a sneaky feeling he'll end up buying more properties over time too.

Summing up

Anthony started investing young. He didn't wait to have an amazing salary, or $100000 in savings. He decided to do everything he could to get his foot in the door, following the 3 golden rules to buy properties he could later refinance to help him make the next purchase. This is possible for you too. This was my story, and many others I know. You do not need to be in your thirties or forties or on an epic salary to become an investor. There is nothing stopping you buying your first property now, expect fear or lack of desire. This book has taught you what you need to know, and there are other resources on my website and YouTube channel if you still have questions. If you've been looking for a sign – this is it! You will NEVER regret investing now. You will only ever regret doing nothing, and having a less great financial future because of it. Get started! You can do it!

CHAPTER 10
Property examples

I know that nothing beats seeing real-life property examples, so in this chapter I'm going to talk you through four properties I've recently bought myself, and six recent purchases I found for my clients. I also highlight two times that I didn't follow my 3 golden rules—and as you might expect, the outcome was less than desirable.

Properties I've bought

I buy about 90 per cent of my properties off-market, but I mainly share properties here that I found online so you can get a feel for what you could find yourself.

BALDIVIS, WESTERN AUSTRALIA

Purchased: February 2023

Price: $557500

Comparable market price: $590000+

(continued)

Why this property was under market price: The owner was struggling to sell.

Rental income and yield: $1000 per week — 9.32 per cent.

Baldivis is on the south side of Perth close to the beach, and you still can drive to Perth CBD in about 30 to 40 minutes. This property was built in around 2016, so I could see it was pretty modern and fresh. It ticks all the boxes.

This is what they call a duplex (or dual occupancy) property. A duplex is basically two properties under one roof. One side is a three-bedroom, two-bathroom, one-car property (a three-two-one for short), and the other is a two-bedroom, one-bathroom, one-car property (a two-one-one). Both were owner-occupied at the time.

The agent was finding it hard to sell. I saw it was on the market for about three or four months; properties like this weren't selling as quickly then as they are now. They wanted $580 000 to $590 000 for it. I checked it out on RP Data; in this particular suburb, a duplex is extremely rare. I called the agent, and we negotiated back and forth.

I could see it had been on the market for months, so I started with $550 000. (The longer a property is on the market, the more ability you have to negotiate. If it had hit the market a week or two prior and they'd had offers already, a lowball offer wouldn't work.) Before making my offer, I made sure to politely let the real estate agent know that I knew it was struggling to sell: 'It's been on the market for three or four months now, if I'm not mistaken. Is that correct?'

They countered with $570000, so I raised my offer by $1000 to $551000, and they came back with $560000. We eventually met at $557500. It settled a couple of months later.

I forecasted that I would be able to rent this property out for a combined rent of about $700 to $750 a week, but my experienced property manager said, 'There's so much demand for properties like this, people are living with family members, let's rent it out as one property.' Sure enough, my property manager was able to easily rent it out for $1000 a week combined, which blew my mind. It was originally listed for $900 a week and we had about seven different offers come in, and then one of them offered $1000 a week to secure it. The yield is 9.32 per cent, which really blew me away. Table 10.1 (overleaf) shows how the numbers stacked up.

(continued)

Table 10.1: cashflow for this property

Estimated expenses	Weekly	Monthly	Annually
Estimated council rates	$45.77	$198.33	$2380.00
Estimated strata fees, including building insurance	$ -	$ -	$ -
Estimated water rates	$24.04	$104.17	$1250.00
Estimated insurance	$25.96	$112.50	$1350.00
Estimated management fees	$57.69	$250.00	$3000.00
Estimated repayments 6.0% interest only	$515.38	$2233.33	$26800.00
Estimated landlord Insurance	$13.46	$58.33	$700.00
Estimated totals	**$682.31**	**$2956.67**	**$35480.00**
Income comparables			
Estimated lower rent	$900.00	$3900.00	$46800.00
Estimated higher rent	$1000.00	$4333.33	$52000.00
Estimated cashflow before tax			
Estimated lower rent	$217.69	$943.33	$11320.00
Estimated higher rent	$317.69	$1376.67	$16520.00

MAYLANDS, WESTERN AUSTRALIA

Purchased: November 2022

Price: $187 000

Comparable market price: $230 000 to $240 000

Why this property was under market price: It was tenanted.

Rental income and yield: $350 per week — 9.73 per cent.

This property was on the market for a little while but was hard to sell because it was tenanted, so the owners ended up taking it off the market because they didn't have to sell it. After buying other properties from the same real estate agent, they said, 'Well, we had this one up for sale and they never ended up selling it. They were originally hoping for about $200 000. Are you interested?'

The tenants were planning to move out at the end of the lease, and it was rented for $265 a week at that time, which was very much under-rented. I could see comparable properties in Maylands were selling for $230 000 to $240 000.

I negotiated with the agent for a couple of days. I offered $185 000 originally, and they countered with $195 000. We ended up meeting in the middle at $187 000.

It's nothing fancy, just a two-bedroom unit four kilometres from the Perth CBD. It's on the ground floor, and close to shops, schools, amenities, train stations, and so on. Once the tenants moved out, I rented the unit for $350 per week, giving it a phenomenal rental yield. Maylands is a suburb where houses sell for a million dollars. Other two-bedroom units in Maylands now sell for around $270 000 to $280 000, so it's gone up nearly a hundred thousand more than the price I paid in less than a year (at the time of writing).

Table 10.2 (overleaf) shows the cashflow breakdown for this property.

(continued)

Table 10.2: cashflow for this property

Estimated expenses	Weekly	Monthly	Annually
Estimated council rates	$28.65	$124.17	$1490.00
Estimated strata fees, including building insurance	$47.12	$204.17	$2450.00
Estimated water rates	$16.92	$73.33	$880.00
Estimated insurance	$ -	$ -	$ -
Estimated management fees	$30.77	$133.33	$1600.00
Estimated repayments 6.0% interest only	$173.08	$750.00	$9000.00
Estimated landlord Insurance	$7.02	$30.42	$365.00
Estimated totals	**$303.56**	**$1315.42**	**$15785.00**
Income comparables			
Estimated lower rent	$340.00	$1473.33	$17680.00
Estimated higher rent	$380.00	$1646.67	$19760.00
Estimated cashflow before tax			
Estimated lower rent	$36.44	$157.92	$1895.00
Estimated higher rent	$76.44	$331.25	$3975.00

This was an affordable property that anyone could get started with. You could buy this with as little as $30 000 in savings, and it could be a stepping stone to more property purchases.

ARCHERFIELD, QUEENSLAND

Purchased: February 2023

Price: $951 000

Comparable market price: $1 050 000

Rental income and yield: $1600 per week — 8.74 per cent.

This property in Brisbane was an urgent auction that I found online and snapped up. It's a full block of four units in Archerfield. It's very close to shops, schools, train

(continued)

stations and other amenities, and it's only 12–13 kilometres from Brisbane's CBD.

I think the owners were coming close to retirement and wanted to cash out of their investment. It's a prime example of a property that only investors would fight over because it's not a singular property, it's a block of four units on what they call a 'single title'. The individual units were not strata titled, meaning there were no strata fees.

I bought this right when interest rates were starting to go through the roof. I saw that a lot of investors were starting to take a step back because they were worried about interest rates going up, which is perfectly normal. I saw this as a good opportunity.

When I saw the listing online, I called the real estate agent and found out that the owner had to sell at auction. It's important to find out key things like whether a property will definitely be selling on the day of the auction. Agents have a way of sometimes explaining things without giving all the information away, but when they say it must be sold on the day, that usually implies the sellers are motivated to sell and there might be a potentially lower reserve than what they've advertised, especially if it's a property like this one that will only appeal to investors.

At the time, I had a pre-approval for around the asking price, and I was trying to buy as many properties as I could. This one stood out because it was a block of four units on one title for under a million dollars, which is very hard to find. They're on a 600-square-metre block, and the land alone in Archerfield was worth around $500 000 to $600 000 at the time.

I ended up buying the unit block at auction. I bid over the phone using one of the representatives that were actually at the auction; they did the bidding on my behalf, following my instructions. If I remember correctly, someone started off at $500000, which was ridiculously low. I was in a rush (it was a Saturday, and my wife was indicating that she wanted me to get off the phone so we could leave the house), so I thought I'd better speed things along. I knew it was going to sell for above $850000, so I bid $750000. Then it was just me and another person battling back and forth. We slowed down at around $880000, switching to very small increases with our bids. Finally, the other bidder offered $950000, I offered $1000 more, and they bowed out.

All four units were rented out at that time of purchase for less than they should be because the owner had self-managed it rather than using a property management company. The rents were the same amount when I bought the block in 2023 as they had been in 2018 – they hadn't gone up in five years. It was originally rented out for a combined amount of roughly $1300 per week, and it's now rented for $1600 per week (across all four). That's an extra $15600 a year in rental income, and giving me an 8.74 per cent yield.

Buying a whole block of units

This Archerfield unit block is the only block of units that I've bought, and I wouldn't buy another one. There are pros and cons for every style of property, but the downside of buying a unit block is that it changes your finance situation. Finance becomes harder to get when you're buying property like unit blocks — many banks see them as risky because they know owner-occupiers aren't going to buy them.

(continued)

The other negative is the size of the deposit required. If you only have a couple of investment properties and you go to buy a unit block, the lender would require a 30 to 40 per cent deposit because banks deem a block of units as commercial lending, which tends to have higher risk. A 35 per cent deposit for this unit block would be $332 850, and by the time you add stamp duty you'd be putting down about three times the amount of cash you might need for another investment. I did a 20 per cent deposit on this block of units because I had equity in other properties, and I used my property management company as collateral. If I had needed to put down a larger deposit, I wouldn't have bought it.

Buying a whole block might stroke your ego, but it's not practical. To me, you're better off buying a couple of houses or units first. I'm unlikely to buy a block like this again. Table 10.3 gives a breakdown of the figures for this property.

Table 10.3: cashflow for this block of units

Estimated expenses	Weekly	Monthly	Annually
Estimated council rates	$55.77	$241.67	$2900.00
Estimated strata fees, including building insurance	$ -	$ -	$ -
Estimated water rates	$53.85	$233.33	$2800.00
Estimated insurance	$40.38	$175.00	$2100.00
Estimated management fees	$103.85	$450.00	$5400.00
Estimated repayments 6.0% interest only	$884.62	$3833.33	$46000.00
Estimated land-lord Insurance	$26.92	$116.67	$1400.00
Estimated totals	**$1165.38**	**$5050.00**	**$60600.00**

Income comparables			
Estimated lower rent	$1400.00	$6066.67	$72800.00
Estimated higher rent	$1600.00	$6933.33	$83200.00

Estimated cashflow before tax			
Estimated lower rent	$234.62	$1016.67	$12200.00
Estimated higher rent	$434.62	$1883.33	$22600.00

CRESTMEAD, QUEENSLAND

Purchased: December 2021

Price: $400 000

Comparable market price: $440 000 to $450 000

Rental income and yield: $480 per week — 6.5 per cent.

This property was a complete off-market sale. I've bought hundreds of properties from the real estate agents who were selling this property. They were selling it on behalf of an investor they knew who was selling a few of their properties to cash out and buy a big place to live in.

This house had been renovated inside, and I bought it for $400 000 right as the market was taking off in Brisbane. It was under-rented at the time, and now rents for $480 per week. The yield is lower because it's a house rather than a unit or apartment.

Around the time I bought this house, I could see that similar properties were selling for $440 000 to $450 000. We negotiated back and forth for a long time. They started at the $420 000 to $430 000 mark, and my first offer was $375 000. We eventually met in the middle at $400 000.

This was one of the last purchases I made in Brisbane as the market started going through a big growth cycle.

The yield back then was 6.5 per cent, which is good for a house. Now, because the market has gone up so much, it wouldn't be worth buying as an investment. You'd have to pay $550 000 to $570 000 for it today, and you'd rent it out for about $500 a week, which is a yield of only 5 per cent. Table 10.4 shows how the figures stacked up for this property.

Table 10.4: cashflow for this property

Estimated expenses	Weekly	Monthly	Annually
Estimated council rates	$36.54	$158.33	$1900.00
Estimated strata fees, including building insurance	$ -	$ -	$ -
Estimated water rates	$21.15	$91.67	$1100.00
Estimated insurance	$21.15	$91.67	$1100.00
Estimated management fees	$28.85	$125.00	$1500.00
Estimated repayments 6.0% interest only	$392.31	$1700.00	$20 400.00
Estimated landlord Insurance	$6.54	$28.33	$340.00
Estimated totals	**$506.54**	**$2195.00**	**$26 340.00**
Income comparables			
Estimated lower rent	$480.00	$2080.00	$24 960.00
Estimated higher rent	$520.00	$2253.33	$27 040.00
Estimated cashflow before tax			
Estimated lower rent	−$26.54	−$115.00	−$1380.00
Estimated higher rent	$13.46	$58.33	$700.00

(continued)

FYI

Property sale prices listed online can be incorrect; agents make mistakes and typos all the time. I've seen a property sale price of $5 900 000 when it should have been $590 000, and another that said the property had previously sold for $29 000 rather than $290 000. Agents will usually input the sale price soon after the contract of sale is signed, which doesn't take into account further reductions or negotiations. Online it says that the Crestmead property I discuss in this section sold for $430 000, when I actually bought it for $400 000. The pest and building inspection reports showed some major issues, so I was able to get $30 000 taken off the sale price.

Properties I've helped clients buy

Now, let's dive into the details of some example properties that my clients have purchased recently.

MIDLAND, WESTERN AUSTRALIA

Purchased: November 2022

Price: $202 000

Comparable market price: $260 000

Rental income and yield: $340 per week — 8.75 per cent.

When originally looking at this property I realised that Perth was about to hit a growth cycle; it was one of the last affordable metro locations. This property is in Midland, about 17-20 kilometres from Perth's CBD. It's an affordable, blue-collar, family-friendly area.

I saw properties similar to this online that had recently sold, and I called roughly six agents I had been building relationships with in Perth to tell them I was after properties like those. Two of the agents had about six properties between them that they were getting ready to put on the market. From simply making a few phone calls, I now had a head start. I found out that two of the sellers were very motivated.

This property is a modern one-bedroom, one-bathroom home with open-plan living and a garage. It's part of a complex, but it has its own off-road entrance. It's about a 500-metre walk to Midland Gate shopping centre, and it is near train stations and schools.

Thirteen years earlier, this property would have sold for around $330 000 to $345 000 off the plan. They were asking for offers around $220 000. I put in an offer before

(continued)

it went online, starting with $185000. We negotiated back and forth and landed on $202000, which was a very good price. Ten months later, that property is worth around $280000. Affordable properties like this cannot even be built for the purchase price today. Table 10.5 gives a breakdown of the numbers for this property.

The sale was completely off-market.

Table 10.5: cashflow for this property

Estimated expenses	Weekly	Monthly	Annually
Estimated council rates	$27.31	$118.33	$1420.00
Estimated strata fees, including building insurance	$50.00	$216.67	$2600.00
Estimated water rates	$16.31	$70.67	$848.00
Estimated insurance	$ -	$ -	$ -
Estimated management fees	$23.08	$100.00	$1200.00
Estimated repayments 5.0% interest only	$153.85	$666.67	$8000.00
Estimated landlord Insurance	$6.90	$29.92	$359.00
Estimated totals	**$277.44**	**$1202.25**	**$14427.00**

Income comparables			
Estimated lower rent	$330.00	$1430.00	$17160.00
Estimated higher rent	$340.00	$1473.33	$17680.00

Estimated cashflow before tax			
Estimated lower rent	$52.56	$227.75	$2733.00
Estimated higher rent	$62.56	$271.08	$3253.00

BALGA, WESTERN AUSTRALIA

Purchased: February 2023

Price: $235 000

Comparable market price: $280 000+

Why this property was under market price: The property was tenanted at the time, so it was hard to get access for inspections.

Rental income and yield: $530 per week — 11.72 per cent.

This property was another off-market purchase I organised for a client.

The Balga area is approximately 11-12 kilometres from Perth CBD — you can drive there in about 20 minutes. It's a humble and affordable suburb. I believe it used to have a bit of a rough reputation, but it's going through gentrification as people are getting priced out of other suburbs and moving to Balga.

To find this property, I called many agents to ask if they had properties they were working on that were similar to ones they had already sold in Balga. After calling 20 to 30 agents, I came across one who knew an owner with other properties in the same block who wanted to sell. They were hoping for around $240 000 to $245 000, but I knew it was worth at least $280 000 based off similar sales in the area. The property was tenanted at the time, so it was hard to access the property for inspections.

It's a two-bedroom, two-bathroom property on a very small block. There are only about eight units in the block, meaning there are no elevators, pools or other expensive things.

I had the feeling that this real estate agent office was the market leader in Balga, with the highest volume of sales, and I could tell that they just wanted to get a deal done quickly.

(continued)

I put in an offer of $233 000 and eventually went up to $235 000. Even at that price it was a phenomenal buy. It's been nearly a year since my client bought it, and it's massively exceeded my expectations. Other units in the same complex are on the market for offers over $300 000, meaning I purchased it at roughly 20 per cent under market value. Table 10.6 shows how the figures stacked up for this property.

Table 10.6: cashflow for this property

Estimated expenses	Weekly	Monthly	Annually
Estimated council rates	$30.00	$130.00	$1560.00
Estimated strata fees, including building insurance	$ -	$ -	$ -
Estimated water rates	$19.23	$83.33	$1000.00
Estimated insurance	$26.92	$116.67	$1400.00
Estimated management fees	$23.08	$100.00	$1200.00
Estimated repayments 5.5% interest only	$298.08	$1291.67	$15 500.00
Estimated landlord Insurance	$7.02	$30.42	$365.00
Estimated totals	**$404.33**	**$1752.08**	**$21 025.00**
Income comparables			
Estimated lower rent	$480.00	$2080.00	$24 960.00
Estimated higher rent	$530.00	$2296.67	$27 560.00
Estimated cashflow before tax			
Estimated lower rent	$75.67	$327.92	$3935.00
Estimated higher rent	$125.67	$544.58	$6535.00

MAYLANDS, WESTERN AUSTRALIA

Purchased: May 2023

Price: $425 000

Comparable market price: $460 000

Rental income and yield: $600 per week — 7.34 per cent.

This property is a very nice and modern unit in Maylands, 10 minutes from Perth's CBD. The agent had tried to sell it but didn't get anywhere; there were tenants living there, so they took it off the market. The sellers unfortunately made a massive mistake in buying this property off the plan, after being recommended to purchase it by a financial advisor. They paid $565 000 for it in 2015. My client bought it for $425 000 eight years later, and rents it out for $600 a week.

They originally wanted $460 000 for it, which was still a good price, but I negotiated back and forth for about a month. The seller became more desperate as the weeks went on, so ended up accepting $425 000. If you look at the sales of brand-new units in Maylands and the surrounding suburbs, they sell for around $650 000 to $700 000. It was a great buy.

A note on financial advisors

Many financial advisors can be sharks; they get a lot of behind-the-scenes commission from the developers who build these types of properties. They might get a $50 000 commission if they tell someone to buy this property: 'It will be a good investment, because if you are earning $X amount, you can claim a lot of tax depreciation.' Sure, it might reduce your income tax bill, but you won't make anywhere near as much as you might have with a smarter property purchase.

(continued)

Luckily, financial advisors are monitored much more closely now. They couldn't get away with this today, but it unfortunately did happen a lot until recently.

Houses versus units

I presented this unit in Maylands to five clients, and the first four clients said no to it.

One client said no because it was a unit: 'I want to start off with a house.'

I explained that we didn't have any houses at the time, and by not buying this, they were basically throwing $50 000 or so out the window. They'd brought emotion into their decision though and were adamant they wanted a house. Even by explaining the financial strategy of not blowing all your budget on houses that probably won't have as good a rental yield, I cannot always change people's minds.

If you're going to have a portfolio of seven or ten properties, then yes—it's nice to have a couple of houses, a townhouse and a few units. But it doesn't matter what order you buy them in: it's only the 3 golden rules that matter.

The fifth client I showed this unit to saw the phenomenal value and went for it. Table 10.7 shows the cashflow sheet for this property.

Table 10.7: cashflow for this property

Estimated expenses	Weekly	Monthly	Annually
Estimated council rates	$30.00	$130.00	$1560.00
Estimated strata fees, including building insurance	$61.54	$266.67	$3200.00
Estimated water rates	$15.38	$66.67	$800.00
Estimated insurance	$ -	$ -	$ -
Estimated management fees	$23.08	$100.00	$1200.00
Estimated repayments 5.5% interest only	$351.92	$1525.00	$18 300.00
Estimated landlord Insurance	$7.02	$30.42	$365.00
Estimated totals	**$488.94**	**$2118.75**	**$25 425.00**
Income comparables			
Estimated lower rent	$500.00	$2166.67	$26 000.00
Estimated higher rent	$520.00	$2253.33	$27 040.00
Estimated cashflow before tax			
Estimated lower rent	$11.06	$47.92	$575.00
Estimated higher rent	$31.06	$134.58	$1615.00

SECRET HARBOUR, WESTERN AUSTRALIA

Purchased: March 2023

Price: $508 000

Comparable market price: $540 000 to $640 000

Rental income and yield: $650 per week – 6.65 per cent.

I bought this house off-market. It's a big house with four bedrooms, two bathrooms and a two-car garage. Prior to it being tenanted, the owners actually lived in the property. The original owners bought the land, built the house, upgraded it with things like a massive outdoor entertainment area, and then they kept it and rented it out. The owners spent a lot of extra money on it because they thought they'd be there forever.

This property was unbelievable value. You can drive to Perth's CBD in under an hour, so it's relatively metro. Secret Harbour is deemed to be a very good growth location, like Rockingham and Kennedy, and it's roughly a five-minute drive to the beach.

At the time of buying it I could see other similar properties selling for $540 000 to $640 000. They originally wanted $520 000, and even at that price it was phenomenal value because of all the extra money they'd spent on it. I knew if the property was vacant it could probably sell for $590 000. But it had tenants in it, and it's hard to sell houses to investors because they don't tend to have the same yield as smaller properties.

I negotiated the purchase price down to $508 000 and the first client I showed it to jumped on it immediately. Six months later the tenants moved out, who were paying $480 a week in rent, and new tenants moved in paying $650 a week. My client couldn't have been happier. Table 10.8 gives a breakdown of the numbers.

Table 10.8: cashflow for this property

Estimated expenses	Weekly	Monthly	Annually
Estimated council rates	$31.73	$137.50	$1650.00
Estimated strata fees, including building insurance	$ -	$ -	$ -
Estimated water rates	$23.08	$100.00	$1200.00
Estimated insurance	$26.92	$116.67	$1400.00
Estimated management fees	$23.08	$100.00	$1200.00
Estimated repayments 5.5% interest only	$429.92	$1863.00	$22356.00
Estimated landlord Insurance	$7.02	$30.42	$365.00
Estimated totals	**$541.75**	**$2347.58**	**$28171.00**

Income comparables

	Weekly	Monthly	Annually
Estimated lower rent	$580.00	$2513.33	$30160.00
Estimated higher rent	$650.00	$2816.67	$33800.00

Estimated cashflow before tax

	Weekly	Monthly	Annually
Estimated lower rent	$38.25	$165.75	$1989.00
Estimated higher rent	$108.25	$469.08	$5629.00

SEVILLE GROVE, WESTERN AUSTRALIA

Purchased: April 2023

Price: $345 000

Comparable market price: $370 000 to $380 000

Rental income and yield: $440 per week — 6.63% per cent.

Seville Grove is only about 30 minutes from the city, and the suburb has shops, schools, train stations, and so on. This three-bedroom house was rented out at the time of sale, which helped us get a good price. It was bought off-market through another agent. The seller wanted $360 000, and we negotiated it down to $345 000. Comparable properties at the time were selling for around $370 000 to $380 000.

I showed this property to a few clients, and I remember the first client said no because it only had one bathroom ... sigh). The client that bought it saw the amazing value. The land alone, which is a 680-square-metre block, would be worth $300 000 to $340 000 alone.

Six months later, you would have had to pay $420 000 to buy it. Table 10.9 shows how the numbers stacked up.

Table 10.9: cashflow for this property

Estimated expenses	Weekly	Monthly	Annually
Estimated council rates	$36.54	$158.33	$1900.00
Estimated strata fees, including building insurance	$ -	$ -	$ -
Estimated water rates	$25.00	$108.33	$1300.00
Estimated insurance	$21.15	$91.67	$1100.00
Estimated management fees	$23.08	$100.00	$1200.00
Estimated repayments 5.5% interest only	$296.31	$1284.00	$15408.00
Estimated landlord Insurance	$7.02	$30.42	$365.00
Estimated totals	**$409.10**	**$1772.75**	**$21273.00**
Income comparables			
Estimated lower rent	$400.00	$1733.33	$20800.00
Estimated higher rent	$440.00	$1906.67	$22880.00
Estimated cashflow before tax			
Estimated lower rent	−$9.10	−$39.42	−$473.00
Estimated higher rent	$30.90	$133.92	$1607.00

MAIDA VALE, WESTERN AUSTRALIA

Purchased: May 2023

Price: $488 000

Comparable market price: $530 000 to $580 000

Rental income and yield: Likely to be up to $650 per week — 6.92 per cent.

This is another off-market sale that I found. It was a deceased estate. It's a large block of 1022 square metres. There was a special condition on the property: the couple selling it wanted to rent it for six months after the sale, paying $450 a week. The normal rent for a property like this is about $550 a week. There was also about $10 000 of work that needed to be done. The people who inherited it simply didn't have the money to do it up before selling it — if they had, they could have sold it for a lot more. Comparable sales at the time were between $530 000 and $580 000. I negotiated the price down to $488 000, and because the property needed a considerable amount of work I knew it only really suited one client of mine as they were based in Western Australia, so I presented it to him and he snapped it up. Table 10.10 shows the figures for this property.

A recent desktop valuation on this property came in at $630 000, and rents have gone up so much that my client will probably get $600 to $650 a week for it when the old owners move out.

Table 10.10: cashflow for this property

Estimated expenses	Weekly	Monthly	Annually
Estimated council rates	$35.38	$153.33	$1840.00
Estimated strata fees, including building insurance	$ -	$ -	$ -
Estimated water rates	$19.62	$85.00	$1020.00
Estimated insurance	$2.50	$10.83	$130.00
Estimated management fees	$30.77	$133.33	$1600.00
Estimated repayments 6.0% interest only	$442.31	$1916.67	$23 000.00
Estimated landlord Insurance	$6.90	$29.92	$359.00
Estimated totals	**$537.48**	**$2329.08**	**$27 949.00**

Income comparables			
Estimated lower rent	$460.00	$1993.33	$23 920.00
Estimated higher rent	$550.00	$2383.33	$28 600.00

Estimated cashflow before tax			
Estimated lower rent	−$77.48	−$335.75	−$4029.00
Estimated higher rent	$12.52	$54.25	$651.00

Properties I've bought that don't meet the 3 golden rules

I have deviated from my own advice twice, and each time it has been a poor investment. I bought both properties with emotion (or with another motivator outside of it being a good investment), and they haven't done well for me.

Mistake #1

A couple of years ago, I liked the idea of having a holiday house on the coast north of where we live in Sydney, so I started looking at what was available. I didn't follow my strategy of getting it under market value with growth and yield, I was just looking for something nice. I bought a property for $1.76 million at the top of the market (for the market price of the time) that was literally across the road from the beach. It's a massive house made up of three completely separate dwellings; it's a triplex-style property. I thought it would work well because I could rent out two of the three, and leave the other vacant for us to use whenever we wanted.

As far as buying holiday homes goes, this was quite a good way to do it because I still had two rental incomes at least. However, we didn't end up using the third dwelling at all, so eventually I decided to rent it out too. And that's where I'm at with it currently, renting out all three dwellings. The yield is not good—it's about 4 per cent, when I usually aim for around 8 per cent for my investments.

Because it's a weird type of property, a triplex, banks won't do a simple desktop valuation to value it, which makes getting equity out of it harder. Plus, because I bought it at the top of the market during the COVID-19 pandemic, when working from home boomed and people were buying more properties near the beach, it hasn't gone up in value very much.

I'm thinking of selling it.

Mistake #2

A few years ago, I bought 11 acres of land in Queensland with a house on it for $810000. I liked the idea of owning some land, so I thought I'd try something different investment-wise. This property is rented out for about $605 a week, which is a yield of 4.17 per cent. but I'm probably going to sell it. The land was good value, but it doesn't fit my investment strategy.

Because it's a unique property, banks won't do a standard desktop valuation to value it—they only do full valuations. Full valuations are usually conservative, so I probably wouldn't get a valuation higher than the purchase price (maybe $850000, best-case scenario). It's a weirdly shaped, huge block.

Cookie-cutter properties that banks do desktop valuations on are the ones to buy: here, a better option would have been a house on a 300- or 400-square-metre block of land, with four bedrooms, two bathrooms and a two-car garage, similar to many others in the same suburb; or a townhouse with three bedrooms, two bathrooms and one car space, similar to other townhouses in the area. They're all the same; they're going to be valued the same, roughly.

When you start buying unique properties, like my triplex by the beach or this amount of acreage—or a house with a granny flat, or a house on a corner block that you could subdivide—they're not easy properties to value and get your equity out of quickly. That doesn't mean it's the end of the world if you buy a place like this, but the low yield does negatively impact the overall cashflow of your whole portfolio. It can be very hard to use these properties to get equity out so you can buy something else, therefore they can really weigh you down.

Summing up

I hope these property examples inspire you to see what's possible! You can own properties like this too. You can become an investor and better yourself financially. I see people do it every day!

Now, let's talk about how to manage a property portfolio.

CHAPTER 11
Managing your portfolio

Buying new properties can be a thrill, but there is of course work that goes into managing them over time. Let's dive into what it looks like to manage your portfolio well, including building the right team of professionals around you to help you do so. Some people like to do a lot of the management themselves, but I recommend outsourcing as much as you can so your portfolio doesn't take up much of your time. I currently have 81 properties, and I spend, on average, eight hours a month managing my portfolio.

Hire the team you need

Building the right team to manage your properties is important. You want to know that they will take good care of the things that you don't have the time, and maybe the expertise, to worry about yourself.

You need the right mortgage broker and the right accountant to manage your portfolio. (And if you plan to set up an SMSF, find an accountant who is really experienced in managing property portfolios as well as SMSFs.) And then, based on where your properties are located, you will either use one or multiple conveyancers and property managers. Conveyancers are only needed when purchasing or selling properties, and mortgage brokers are only needed when purchasing or refinancing properties. Your accountant and property managers will do the bulk of the management work month in, month out to keep your portfolio ticking along nicely. In chapter 5, I talk about how to find a mortgage broker that's best for you, and how to find a conveyancer too.

When it comes to finding an accountant, choose one who's an investor themselves. That's one of the biggest indicators that they will do a good job for you. Ask the accountants you're considering if they own any properties themselves, and if they have clients that own five or 10 properties. If they have clients in the same position as you, they'll know how to do your tax returns and so on properly.

Finding good property managers

Having good property managers will make your life as an investor easy, and having bad ones will cause you unnecessary work, which is very frustrating. A property manager's job is to manage the property for you, so they should do almost everything, making your life easy and relatively stress-free. When something breaks at the property they'll let you know, and ideally will already have a solution lined up for you.

For example, you might get a call along the lines of, 'Hi, just calling to let you know the hot water service has stopped working. Given the unit is 10 years old, would you like to replace it, or should I call a serviceman out to fix it for you? We have people we can recommend for you to either repair or replace it.' And then, when you've decided what you'd prefer, they organise it for you, and they pay the tradespeople out of the rent money they collect on your behalf. (I talk about how to choose and deal with property managers in chapter 5.)

Property management is not an easy job, and it's very hard for any property manager to make zero mistakes. Even good property managers will have hiccups happen on their watch, and it's best to go into property investing knowing and expecting that things may happen that require your attention.

Unlike accountants and mortgage brokers—who can be based anywhere and still work with you—property managers have to work in the same or a neighbouring suburb of where your property is located. So, if you're buying properties in different locations, you need to find a new property manager every time you purchase in a new area. Unfortunately, the hiring process is often trial and error—some are good, and some are bad. I move around to find the good ones, and when I find good property managers, I stay with them.

If you have friends that are investors in the same area, they will (hopefully) know of great property managers they can refer you to. Nowadays I do this for clients, matching them up with good property managers who I personally use and recommend. It's much easier than calling up 10 different property managers and hoping you choose the right one. But if you don't have anyone who can make recommendations for you, you're going to have to use trial and error until you find a good property manager.

Offloading the admin work

Some people like to do all the admin for their properties themselves, from paying the council rates through to paying the plumber who the property manager called out to fix a tap. Some people may even organise the repairs themselves. When you only have one property, it can be tempting to manage the admin yourself so you're in control and know how much is being spent. But the admin side of things is actually a whole lot of work that you don't have to do.

Every month you pay your property manager the same amount of money, regardless of whether you or they do this work—so use them! Be sure to make the most of your team when you have a few properties under your belt and the admin work increases. Offload as much admin as you can to your property manager. They can sort out paying council rates, water rates, management fees and strata bills. You simply redirect these bills to your property manager's office, and they will open and pay those bills on your behalf from your rental income. You never have to see the bills nor actually pay them manually yourself—and if you want to be across everything, you can simply track your income and outgoings in relation to your properties via Property Rental Statements (that you receive from the property managers every two to four weeks).

With my first seven or eight properties, I did all the admin myself—and it was the biggest nightmare keeping on top of it. You can have someone else worry about it all for you at no additional cost. Do it.

Trusting your rental management company

It can feel like a big deal to hand over responsibility for your rental income and properties to your property managers, but rest assured that there is a lot in place to protect landlords.

Every fortnight you'll receive a statement from your property manager that shows all the rent that has been collected, all the fees that have been deducted from that rent and what's left over for you.

All the rent goes into the property manager's real estate office's trust account. Trust accounts are audited every year. If a dollar goes missing from it, or gets put in the wrong place, the real estate agent can lose their licence very easily and be fined massive amounts. There are strict legal processes in place to monitor the way your money is managed.

Personally, I'm not worried about theft. You can literally check your statement from your property manager every fortnight—and review what money is hitting your bank account to check it matches up with what you're expecting—as often as you want to. (Perhaps set a reminder in your calendar to check it once a month or once a quarter—however often you feel comfortable with.)

Getting involved with maintenance and repairs

If you'd like your property manager to run every maintenance request past you, you can ask them to do so, but if you don't have the time to deal with every single request (especially when you have several properties), you can give your property manager a price point up to which you don't want to be bothered for requests for maintenance or repairs. They then have the authority to sort issues out without bothering you. You can find out how much money is being spent on maintenance and repairs on a regular basis from your fortnightly statement so you don't clock up a surprising repair bill over time (for example, seeing a $150 charge because the property manager had to send a tradie out to fix a leaking tap).

When I started letting my property manager handle maintenance and repairs on my behalf, I asked that they didn't bother me with the decision if the cost was under $250, which gave them the authority to go ahead and organise for any repairs or replacements to be made. (One time a property manager called me up about a new gas cylinder needing to be installed for $79. I told them to just get it done!) When you only have a couple of properties you may prefer for them to call you every time, but as your portfolio grows you will soon tire of receiving those calls—trust me.

I own 81 properties now; imagine if I got a call for every single maintenance request that came through from my tenants! To make things even easier, I have increased my original budget ceiling from $250 to $700. So all of my property managers have the authority to decide on repairs that come in for under $700. I said to them, 'Do the best thing—whether something needs to be replaced or repaired, just organise it.'

Maybe to start with, when you only have one property, you'll choose that if it's under $100, you don't want to be bothered with it, and you can increase the amount to $300, $400 or $500 as you go.

Sometimes, an exceptional circumstance might arise that means the difference between a call-out fee or cheap repair that doesn't deliver the required outcome, or an expensive (but necessary) replacement fee—for example, the time my property manager called me because the air conditioner stopped working in one of my rental properties. They said, 'Look, we can either send someone out there to check it, and it'll be a $150 call-out fee for them just to see if they can repair it, or instead they can supply and instal a new one, which will cost $1900.' In that instance, I decided that because the air-con unit wasn't old (it was only five or six years old), it was better to risk a $150 call-out fee and see if they could repair it with a simple fix rather than pay nearly two grand to get a new one. However, if it had been a 20-year-old air-con unit, I would have asked the property manager to arrange for a new one to be installed.

With decisions like that, which require a financial weigh-up, I ask my property managers to email me the two options rather than call me, because it's helpful to have more time to digest the information so I can make a good decision. You don't want to spend unnecessary cash on replacements, but you don't want to be penny-wise but pound-foolish either. However, if the highest cost option is under $700, I am now comfortable with letting my property managers make the decision for me. I ask them to do what they would do if the property was theirs. (This is why it's worth shopping around until you find good property managers!)

Choose a rental price to keep good tenants

I touched on rental prices in chapter 2, but I want to discuss it more fully here as it's an important part of life as an investor. How much rent should you charge? When should you put the rent up, and by how much? I think too many investors jack up their rents to the very highest amount they can get, which can lead to tenants moving out in search of cheaper rentals—which then costs you in terms of loss of rent between tenants. So, is increasing the rent really worth it?

For example, if I was trying to get an extra $20 a week from a property, sure, over a year that might be an extra $1000 roughly in my pocket. But if the tenants move out and I have to get a new tenant, I then have to pay my property manager the fee to get it re-tenanted, plus it might sit empty for a week or two.

Letting fees (the costs of finding a new tenant) can be as much as two weeks' rent in itself, or more. So, for a $400 per week rental, you might have to pay $800 for the letting fee, not to mention the advertising cost, and then the property might be vacant for a week between tenants, which is another $400. So it could end up costing you $1400 to find new tenants, and you're only going to get an extra $1000 a year in rent. If the tenants choose to move out because of the increase, you're losing money on that decision.

Plus, when a property is vacant, that's usually when a property manager will say, 'Well, given it's empty right now, it's actually worth repainting the property, you'll get more rent then.' And now you're deciding whether you want to spend money on repainting the place, and while you're at it maybe replacing the carpet too. All of which might not have needed to be done for another couple of years if you'd kept those tenants in and happy. Maybe there are similar properties to yours renting out for $20 to $50 more a week, but often it's a better financial decision to not risk the re-letting costs.

In the past, media interviewers have tried to make me look like a bad guy for increasing rents in the properties I own, so I sent them evidence showing that roughly 90 per cent of my properties are under-rented compared to what they could be getting. They could be rented out for $10 to $30 a week more, but under-renting is worth it to ensure they're always rented out and that tenants stay for longer – it's much better to need to find new tenants every three to five years, as opposed to every year or two.

All that said, there are times when it is okay to increase the rent. Generally, you do so when a lease finishes. If your property is under-rented based on comparable properties in the area, of course you'll want to put the rent up. Again, I wouldn't go for the max you think you could get; I would put it up so it's still around $20 a week less than other properties. If you buy a property with tenants on a fixed lease that is clearly under-rented, when the lease ends you'll definitely need to increase it. You can ask the property manager to kindly point out to the tenants how much comparable properties are renting for so they realise how good a deal they've had, which will usually make them accept the rental increase with more goodwill. For example, if your property is currently rented for $350 a week, and comparable properties are renting for $480 a week, asking your property manager to point this out to your tenants before telling them their rent will increase to $450 a week increases the chance they will appreciate that you're still giving them a discount rather than charging them the $480 you could be charging.

You particularly want to do this if the tenants are really good and you know they want to stay. The property manager simply needs to say, 'Other similar units are on the market for $480 to $500 a week. We want you to stay in here, so we're only putting the rent up to $450 a week.'

You obviously need to act in the best interest of your investment. If the rent can be increased, put it up within reason. I'm personally fine with it being $20 a week under the market median price to get tenants to stay. Do what you can to minimise vacancies. Make it a win-win situation.

Different ways to refinance

Most of my clients will refinance some of their properties (some refinance them all) to help them grow their portfolio faster. I've discussed refinancing properties in Kate's story (chapters 5 to 7), but let's dive into more of the details here.

One of the main ways to increase how quickly you can buy more properties is to refinance existing properties and use the equity from them for deposits and closing costs. To refinance, you can either go directly to the bank, or you can go through a mortgage broker.

It's a lot easier to refinance with a mortgage broker because they can use their online platform to get you multiple desktop valuations from different banks all at once, so you can choose the best option. Only brokers can do this. They have to be qualified and set up in the banks' internal systems with login credentials to do the desktop valuations. Your broker will use the banks' own internal valuing systems that estimate property values based off sales data and information from RP Data. This means the broker can order a desktop valuation from (for example) NAB, St.George Bank or Westpac, and the software will generate valuations from each bank. All the valuations will vary, which is why it's so helpful having a broker to do this all at once for you—you can then decide which bank is the best for your situation. If you personally go from one bank to another yourself, it will take a lot longer and it won't be as clear which is the best bank to go with.

If you bought a property for $300000 and you think it's worth $350000 or more, your mortgage broker can order multiple desktop valuations with multiple banks and let you know that one came in at $330000, two came in at $350000 and one came in at $380000. The decision is clear: go with the bank that valued the property at $380000. (Unless their interest rate is significantly higher, your mortgage broker will guide you through the other details so you can make the best decision.)

However, there are times when going directly to the bank is a good idea. When I owned a few properties I felt stuck for three or six months, which felt like an eternity. I was going to different brokers who were all saying it was too difficult to get equity out of my properties, or that I could only get about $30000 of equity out. I went to multiple brokers who did multiple valuations, and all came back saying it wasn't possible to refinance. Eventually I walked across the road to a bank, booked in a consultation with one of the brokers there and refinanced three properties in one go within

48 hours (which normally would have taken at least a month for a mortgage broker to do). That's when I learned that brokers don't always have access to the same internal valuations that banks do.

In this case, the bank had access to a different valuation system that the brokers didn't have. At that particular time, the bank's valuations came in higher than the normal valuations (via the broker) did. The brokers couldn't see that the valuation would come in higher if I went to the bank directly.

So though I usually recommend using a broker, if that avenue is not working for you speak to a few banks directly to see what they can offer you. If you don't have luck refinancing one way, there are almost always other options.

Three ways to use equity

There are three main ways to use equity to fund the purchase of future properties: cross collateralisation, loan top-ups and side loans. I regularly do both loan top-ups and side loans, though a top-up loan is usually the easiest way to refinance—and I have used all three options. You can use any and all of them depending on what you need and what works best for you. Here's a rundown of what each way of using equity entails.

Cross collateralisation

Cross collateralisation is a finance term describing when you use an asset to secure a new loan. For example, you own a property that has a mortgage on it, and that property is obviously the collateral for that loan. Now you want to buy another property, and rather than refinancing to take equity out of your first property, you use the first property as collateral for the new loan as well (allowing you to borrow the full purchase price of the new property). What you're doing is tying the loans together, which means if you can't pay the mortgage repayments on one loan, the lender will usually sell both of your properties to recoup their money. Cross collateralisation limits your flexibility when you want to refinance to a different bank because both loans are tied to the second property, so you can't move one loan to another bank. The benefit is that the loan on the original property doesn't increase as you haven't taken the equity out of that property, you've simply used that property as collateral for the new property.

I don't recommend cross collateralisation because of the inflexibility and added risk it creates, plus tying the loans together throws out the loan to value ratios (LVRs) of both properties. In other words, if you need to sell one property, the lender has to untie the properties—and they will only do this if the LVRs of each property can stand alone.

To explain this further, let's say you have Property 1, which is valued at $350 000, and the loan is $300 000. If you then buy Property 2 for $200 000 using Property 1 as collateral, the loan is $200 000 (100 per cent of the purchase price). Two years later, you want to sell Property 1, which is now valued at $420 000. But Property 2 is only valued at $210 000, meaning you only have $10 000 in equity you can take out on Property 2, which the bank probably won't think is enough. To untie the loans, you will need to use equity from Property 1 to pay off more of Property 2—enough to get Property 2 to the point that its LVR is good enough for it to stand alone.

Banks are usually happy to do cross collateralisation because it keeps you from refinancing elsewhere. A bank got me to use my equity this was with my first two properties when I didn't even understand what cross collateralisation was, and it was unhelpful for my investment strategy. Only cross collateralise if it's a worst-case scenario and you have no other choice.

Loan top-up

Another way to use the equity from your property is to do a loan top-up. This is where you borrow against the equity of a property that you already own. This is what Kate did to afford buying more properties, and it's what many of my clients (and myself) do.

So, if your original loan for a $300000 property was $270000 but the property is now worth $350000, the lender can increase your loan by $45000 to $315000 (if you're happy with an LVR of 90 per cent). This $45000 in equity (minus lenders' mortgage insurance, or LMI) is deposited into your bank account in cash, which you can then put towards your next property purchase. Of course, your monthly mortgage payments will increase because your loan amount has increased, so before doing this you need to calculate if the rental income of your property will cover the new monthly repayment amount.

Side loan

An equity side loan is similar to a loan top-up, but instead of your existing loan increasing by $45000 minus LMI (and that amount being put into your bank account in cash), there is a new side loan of $45000 set up from which you can withdraw the $45000. It is like a line of credit.

The loan top-up and side loan have the same end result: you have $45000 (minus LMI) that you can access and spend — the difference is in how the lender structures the loan. Either your original loan is increased, or the original loan stays the same and a separate side loan is attached.

The main benefit of doing a side loan rather than a top-up loan is for tax purposes. If, for example, the house you live in is worth a million dollars and the loan on it is $500000, and you want to access $100 000 of its equity to invest in property, it's better to attach a side loan to your current mortgage, because then it is tax deductible. If you did a loan top-up, increasing the loan on your primary place of residence to $600 000, you can't make use of the tax deduction.

Summing up

Managing your property portfolio yourself could be a lot of work if you choose to do it that way ... or you can set things up in a way that makes it a lot less work for you every month. I highly recommend doing this! The more properties you buy, the more the workload increases. Outsource everything you can, and remember that you can still keep a watchful eye over everything to check it's being managed how you want.

CONCLUSION

I hope you've enjoyed reading this book, and I hope that becoming a property investor feels possible for you now. It truly is an option for anyone. If I could do it, growing up with a single mum living off the pension, with no one in my family owning a property, then believe me — you can do it too. Yes, it might take some short-term sacrifice to save up your first deposit, but it's worth it. Once you pass that hurdle and buy your first property following the 3 golden rules, you can keep buying.

And remember, you haven't missed the boat — there are *so* many good deals every single month. In the good times, the bad times, the low or high interest rates, there are good deals. All you need to do is make sure you snap one up for yourself to get started.

I'm passionate about demystifying property investing. If you'd like to learn more, or chat to my team about us finding a property for you, go to www.dilleenproperty.com.au. There you can find out how we can help and what the process is.

If you enjoyed reading this book, please leave a review on Google and Amazon — it really helps others find this book. It would mean the world to me.

I wish you all the success with your investment journey. May you retire earlier, or live a more lavish life, as a result of your hard work now! It pays off.

Eddie

INDEX

Printed and bound by CPI Group (UK) Ltd, Croydon, CR0 4YY

01/03/2024

14461255-0001